D0297981

Ferrari 275GTB

Collectors'
CARS
TIGER BOOKS INTERNATIONAL
LONDON

Editor Julian Brown
Art Editor Trevor Vertigan
Production Richard Churchill

This edition published in 1990 by
Tiger Books International PLC, London

Produced by Marshall Cavendish Books Limited
58 Old Compton Street
London W1V 5PA

Fist printing 1985
5 6 7 8 9   99 98 97 96 95 94 93 92 91 90

ISBN 1 85501 044 5

Printed and bound in Portugal

CONTENTS

Ferrari Superfast

INTRODUCTION

Many cars built since the end of the Second World War have now joined their illustrious predecessors in the car collections and museums of the world. This does not just apply to the expensive and exclusive cars such as those produced by Rolls-Royce and Lincoln. As with many other mass-produced items like glass bottles and cast-iron manhole covers, everyday products have become sought after and cherished in a way that would astonish their original designers and makers.

Some of this appeal is due to nostalgia. The shortcomings of a car can get overlooked because it represents the youth of an individual or a period of time that appears to be happier and more satisfying than our own. This view may be quite mistaken, but careful analysis cannot dispel the attraction of cars like the MGA. Let the experts declare that it was slow and uncomfortable — the lines, the handling and the spirit are enough to explain its appeal to thousands who never drove one.

While not an exhaustive study, this first section reviews the various parts of the motor car with an account of how each component has developed through many dead ends to its modern combination of reliability, economy and ease of manufacture.

Lamborghini Miura

Even the cheapest cars of today compare favourably with the best cars of the '30s in terms of comfort and performance. In order to achieve this improvement, each component has been subjected to a process of testing and refinement that has transformed it. Other items, like heaters, have proceeded from being 'extras' that had to be paid for to standard items without which no car goes on the road. It even applies to humble components like the starter and the generator. For without the increased electrical output of the alternator and the improved engagement of the pre-engaged starter the extraordinary reliability and comfort of the modern car would not be possible.

The post-war period started with cars built without heaters, unless you owned something like a Mk 6 Bentley. By the early '50s heaters were an optional extra, though you can still buy heaters to fit yourself as an afterthought. By the '60s, the heater was an integral part of the design and it was unthinkable for any car to be produced without one.

These years cover the period in which people stopped laying-up their cars every winter and started to expect them to start reliably at any temperature. That is the measure of the progress.

ENGINE POWER

All cars and motor cycles in current production are powered by internal combustion engines, in which the force needed to propel the vehicle is generated inside the engine itself.

Internal combustion engines used in motor vehicles are of two main types. The first is the spark-ignition engine, in which fuel vapour mixed with air is ignited by an electric spark, and the expansion of the air caused by the heat of the combustion is used to drive a piston or rotor; they are usually fuelled by petrol.

The second type is the compression-ignition engine, which also uses the heat from a combustion process to drive a piston, but in which no spark is needed. Instead, the fuel is vaporized and injected into air which has been heated to a temperature at which the fuel becomes self-igniting. Compression-ignition engines use heavy fuel oil rather than petrol.

The force which drives either type of engine is not, strictly speaking, an 'explosion'. The fuels used ignite readily, but burn relatively slowly as compared with, say, dynamite. This characteristic allows the piston to be pushed down its cylinder without damage, unlike with an explosion.

The vast majority of internal combustion engines used in motor vehicles are of the reciprocating type, in which the up-and-down movement of a piston or pistons is converted by means of a crankshaft into a rotary motion—in much the same way that the more-or-less vertical movement of a cyclist's legs is used to rotate a cycle's chain wheel.

Reciprocating engines, in turn, are of two types. In the two-stroke engine, driving force is imparted to the piston once for every revolution of the crankshaft (or two strokes of the piston). In the four-stroke engine, force is imparted once for every two revolutions of the crankshaft (or four strokes of the piston).

In 1984 the TWR Jaguar XJ12C works team won the European Saloon Car Championship. The car was powered by the famous Jaguar V12

Cutaway of the engine that powered Henry Ford's best selling car, the Model T

To obtain work from combustion, the source of the combustion must be confined and its energy directed. Putting a match to a saucer of petrol would produce a 'whoosh' as it caught fire—but little else, because the energy generated by the burning would be dissipated in all directions.

So the basic part of an automobile engine is a cylinder, machined from the engine block so that it is closed at the top. Inside the cylinder is a closely-fitting piston which acts as a seal for the lower part of the cylinder so that the force of the combustion is fully contained. At the same time. the piston is free to move up and down.

Each time combustion takes place, the piston is driven downwards and its motion is transmitted by a connecting rod to a rotating crankshaft. From there the motion is directed, via the vehicle's gearing and transmission system, to the driving wheel or wheels.

The top of the cylinder is not totally sealed at all times, however. Two (sometimes four) openings permit the ingress of fuel and the expulsion of exhaust gases resulting from combustion. These orifices are opened and shut at appropriate intervals by valves, whose movement is controlled by a camshaft driven (indirectly) by the crankshaft. This ensures that the frequency at which fuel is ingested by the cylinder matches the speed of the engine. Another device, the distributor, is also driven by the engine to ensure that the charges of fuel are ignited at the correct intervals.

All reciprocal engines must be started by an outside agency, such as a self-starter motor, kick starter or (on older cars) a starting handle supplied as a defence against self-starter failure. From that point the operation of four-stroke and two-stroke machines is somewhat different.

Four-stroke engine

The four-stroke spark-ignition engine used in the majority of modern motor vehicles was invented—twice—in the 19th century.

The first inventor, in about 1862, was the Frenchman Alphonse Beau de Rochas. The second, about 1875, was the German Dr N. A. Otto. Since neither knew of the other's patent until engines were being manufactured in both countries, a lawsuit followed. De Rochas won a sum of money, but Otto emerged with the fame: the principle of the four-stroke engine is still known as the 'Otto cycle'.

In any reciprocal engine, the two extreme positions between which a piston can move are called top dead centre (TDC) and bottom dead centre (BDC). In a four-stroke engine, each piston starts its pattern of work from TDC. As it begins its first downwards movement, an inlet valve in the top of the cylinder opens to admit petrol vapour mixed with air. By the time the piston has reached BDC it has induced, or sucked in, a full measure of this fuel. This first movement is therefore the induction (or inlet) stroke.

During the next—upwards—stroke, the inlet valve is closed while the piston compresses the fuel mixture so that it will readily ignite. This stroke is therefore known as the compression stroke.

As the piston approached TDC, an electric charge jumps between the electrodes of the spark-plug and ignites the fuel vapour concentrated in the top of the cylinder. The resulting combustion, in which the temperature of the burning fuel can reach 2,000°C and the force, as much as 2 tonnes, drives the piston downwards— the power stroke.

By the time the piston has again reached the bottom of the cylinder, the force of the combustion has been expended. All that remains is to allow the waste products of combustion to escape into the exhaust system and hence into the atmosphere. So at

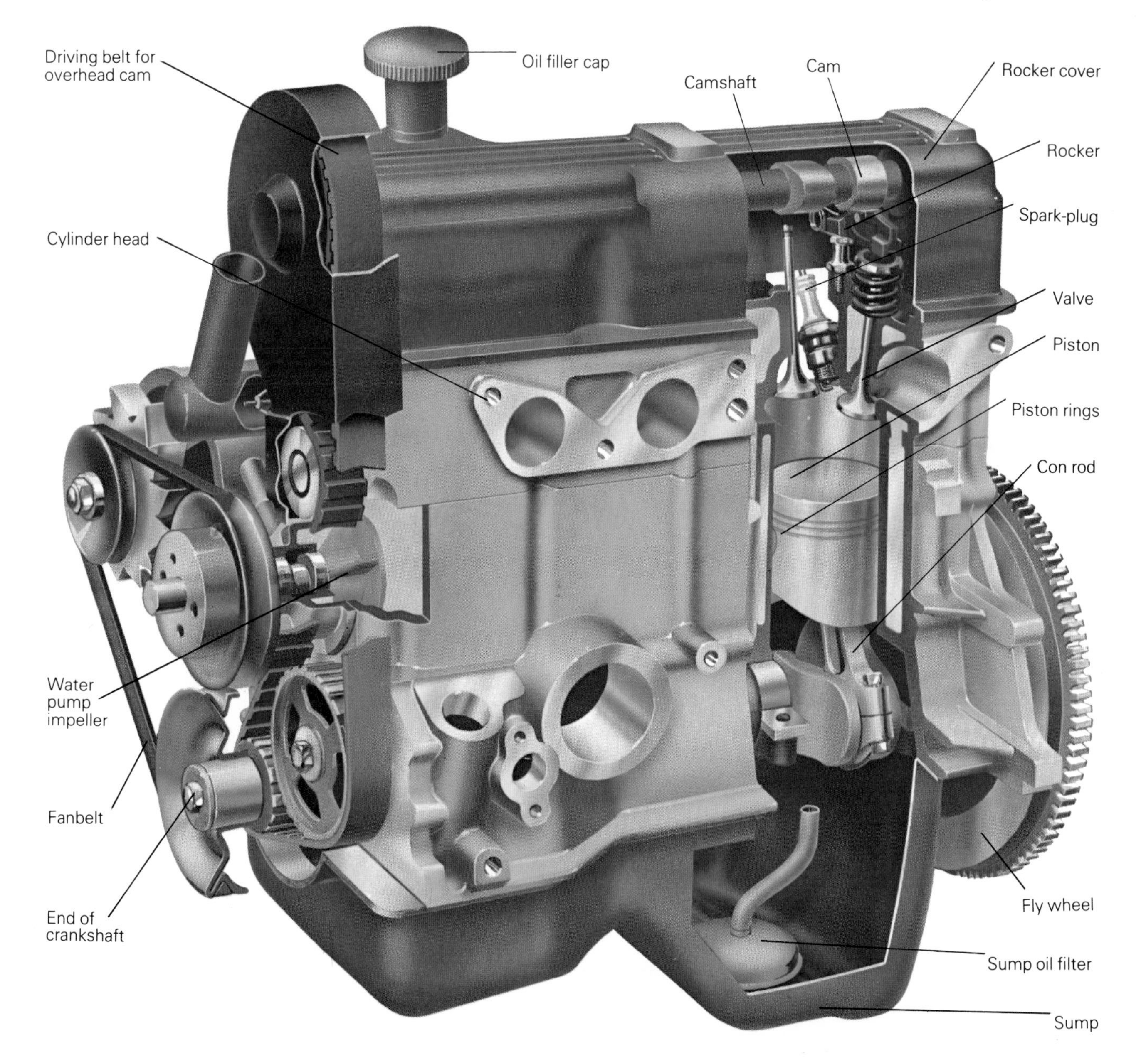

Cutaway of a typical four-stroke car engine, showing its principal components

Testa Rossa is a famous name in Ferrari history, applied to sports-racing cars in the 1950s and a supercar of the 1980s, but actually springing from the red-painted cylinder heads of the classic V12

this stage a second valve in the cylinder, the exhaust valve, opens. This allows the piston on its fourth, or exhaust, stroke to push the gases out through the top of the cylinder.

That is the theory of the four-stroke operation, but in practice the different stages are not as neatly separated as the theory suggests. For example, the engine will generate maximum power if combustion is at its peak when the piston is at the top of its stroke. But burning is not instantaneous; instead, it begins in the fuel mixture that is nearest the spark plug and fans outwards until all the fuel is burned. To allow for this delay, ignition has to take place a fraction of a second—or a few degrees of crankshaft rotation—before the piston reaches TDC.

Similarly, there is a delay between the instant that a valve begins to open and that at which fuel vapour, or exhaust gas, can flow through it at full pressure. So both inlet and exhaust valves are often made to open a few degrees early (a process called valve lead) or close a few degrees late (called valve lag) to increase the engine's efficiency. Such intervals are, of course, only fractions of a second, since even at idling speed a piston in a typical family car moves upwards or downwards about 1,600 times a minute.

Although the piston has to make four movements to complete one cycle of work, the shape of the crankshaft means that each piston can make only two strokes—one upwards, one downwards—for each revolution of the crankshaft itself. So any one piston can apply driving force to the crankshaft only once every four strokes, or two revolutions.

It is perfectly feasible to maintain the turning momentum of the crankshaft between power strokes by means of a flywheel or similar device, and hence to build a four-stroke engine with only one cylinder. But the vibration set up by the spasmodic firing of such an engine would impose an excessive load on both the engine itself and on the vehicle as a whole. Rather than having one huge cylinder, therefore, four-stroke car engines usually have four or more smaller ones which fire in rotation.

Two-stroke engine

Since the four-stroke engine was seen to be relatively inefficient, delivering only one power stroke in four, inventors sought a way of improving it. By 1878 a Scot, Dugald Clerk, developed an engine whose work cycle was completed in two strokes, using a secondary cylinder and piston to feed the fuel mixture into the main cylinder. In 1891 Joseph Day modified Clerk's engine to dispense with the second cylinder, substituting instead an airtight crankcase through which the fuel could be fed on its way to the firing chamber. But the basic principle of the two-stroke engine is still called, after its original inventor, the Clerk cycle.

The two-stroke engine has a cylinder, piston, crankshaft and spark plug as does its four-stroke counterpart. But there are no valves. Instead, three holes—the inlet, exhaust and transfer ports—are cut into the cylinder itself and are blocked or left open by the piston as it moves up and down.

The two-stroke engine must accomplish induction, combustion and exhaust in one up-and-down movement of the piston. The work cycle starts with the piston rising from DBC to uncover the inlet port, thereby inducing a charge of fuel into the airtight crankcase. As the piston continues to rise, it seals off the exhaust and transfer ports and completes the compression of the fuel mixture in the combustion chamber.

Just before TDC, the mixture is ignited and the piston is pushed downwards. As it descends it uncovers the exhaust port to allow the burned gases to escape. At the same time, the bottom part of the piston acts as a pump to force the mixture in the crankcase up the transfer port and into the combustion chamber ready for ignition.

The head of the piston is shaped to reduce the amount of unburned fuel vapour that can mix with the exhaust gases while the piston is around BDC. And, in modern two-stroke engines, the transfer port is shaped to direct the fuel vapour towards the top of the cylinder, away from the exhaust port. But some mixing of unburned and burned gases in inevitable.

Because each piston produces a power stroke for every revolution of the crankshaft, a two-stroke engine should theoretically be twice as powerful as a four-stroke engine of the same dimensions. In practice it is rarely more than 1½ times as powerful.

The NSU Spyder **(bottom)** *was the first commercially successful car to be powered by the Wankel rotary engine* **(below)**

The world-famous Ford Cosworth DFV engine powered Formula One cars to over 150 Grand Prix wins and in its turbocharged DFX form dominated US Indycar racing in the 1980s

There are a number of reasons. One is that the induction and transfer ports are unalterable openings whose whose band of operating efficiency is relatively narrow. If the ports are designed so that a large amount of fuel is used, the engine will tend to work well only at high speeds. If on the other hand the ports are designed for small amounts of fuel, the engine will perform well at low speeds but badly at high. Further, because the piston moves twice as quickly as it would need to in a four-stroke engine of similar revolutions-per-minute, it is subjected to greater heat—but its extra role as a port sealer requires that it be manufactured and maintained to closer tolerances. So higher wear than in a four-stroke is inevitable—damaging performance.

Finally, in spite of advances in design, it is impossible to prevent some of the unburned fuel vapour from mixing with the exhaust gases as it drives them through the exhaust port. As well as wasting petrol and increasing pollution, this can cause deposits of oil to foul the exhaust port and spark plug.

TURBOCHARGING

The energy crisis of the 1970s underlined the need to develop more economical engines and so partly inspired renewed interest in turbochargers. The thermal efficiency of an internal combustion engine is only about 25 per cent; this means that only a small part of the potential energy of the petrol is converted into power. A great deal of energy is rejected down the exhaust pipe, and the turbocharger can harness this, making the engine more efficient, as well as producing more power from a given engine size.

A turbocharger is essentially an exhaust-driven supercharger. A supercharger forces more fuel into the engine than would normally reach it. A turbocharger does exactly the same job. Only the means of driving it is different. A turbocharger has a small turbine and the exhaust gases are channelled through it. This makes the turbine rotate at great speed (speeds of 100,000 rpm are usual).

The turbine is linked by a shaft to a compressor, which is a wheel with a dozen or more curved blades.

So as the turbine spins, the compressor also revolves and the curved blades scoop up air from the intake port. The compressor whirls the air round and it emerges flowing very fast indeed. It then enters a diffuser, which is generally located in the compressor housing.

The diffuser works like a funnel in reverse—it slows down the air, but increases the pressure.

Now at increased pressure, the air is boosted down the induction system, through the carburettor (where it picks up a large charge of petrol) and into the engine.

The fact that the air/fuel mixture is at a high pressure means that more of the mixture rushes into the engine than it can at normal atmospheric pressure. With more fuel in the engine, more power is developed so the turbocharger gives a significant boost to the engine's power output.

The rate of boost given to the engine is regulated by the exhaust. As the exhaust output rises, the turbine and compressor speed both increase.

The exhaust is a source of power that is normally completely wasted, so the turbocharger is a very efficient addition to the engine. Although the turbocharger sounds fairly simple, in reality it requires careful design and manufacture. The application of a turbocharger to a particular engine is seldom simple and the detailed design of the compressor is always particularly complex.

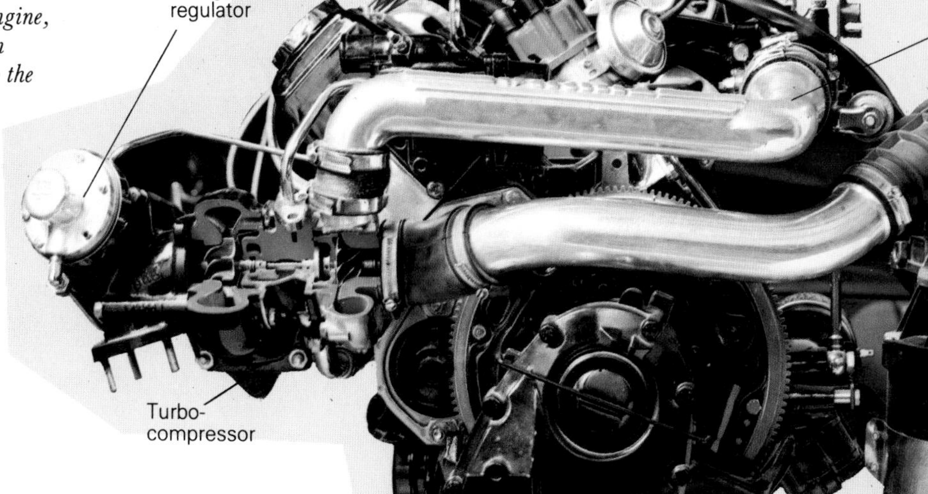

The Saab turbocharged engine, which was a forerunner in bringing turbocharging to the family saloon

Design and development

The design of turbochargers originally owed more to the world of aero engines than to automotive engineering. Compressors and turbines are, in fact, the major components of the jet engine. It is therefore not surprising that the world's largest manufacturer of turbochargers is Garrett AiResearch, who also make gas turbine engines for aircraft.

For road use, the development of turbos originally centred on the larger diesel engines for use in heavy lorries. So the limited supply of suitable components delayed the development of turbocharged petrol engines for cars.

The design of the compressor is probably the most important consideration. The position of the blades on the compressor wheel must be calculated to produce useful boost at the required engine speed. This is a question of careful design of the shape and angle of the blades. The design must also avoid the problem of surging, which can occur at certain speeds when the flow of air about to leave the compressor is reversed. This can wreck the compressor.

When the compressor characteristics have been

Left: *The Brabham BT53, which was moderately successful in the 1984 Grand Prix season, showing a common problem with the BMW turbo engine (which powered the similar BT52 to the 1983 championship)*

Below: *An early supercharger of a pre-war Alfa Romeo 6C. Supercharging, another way of boosting engine power, was overtaken by the development of the turbo*

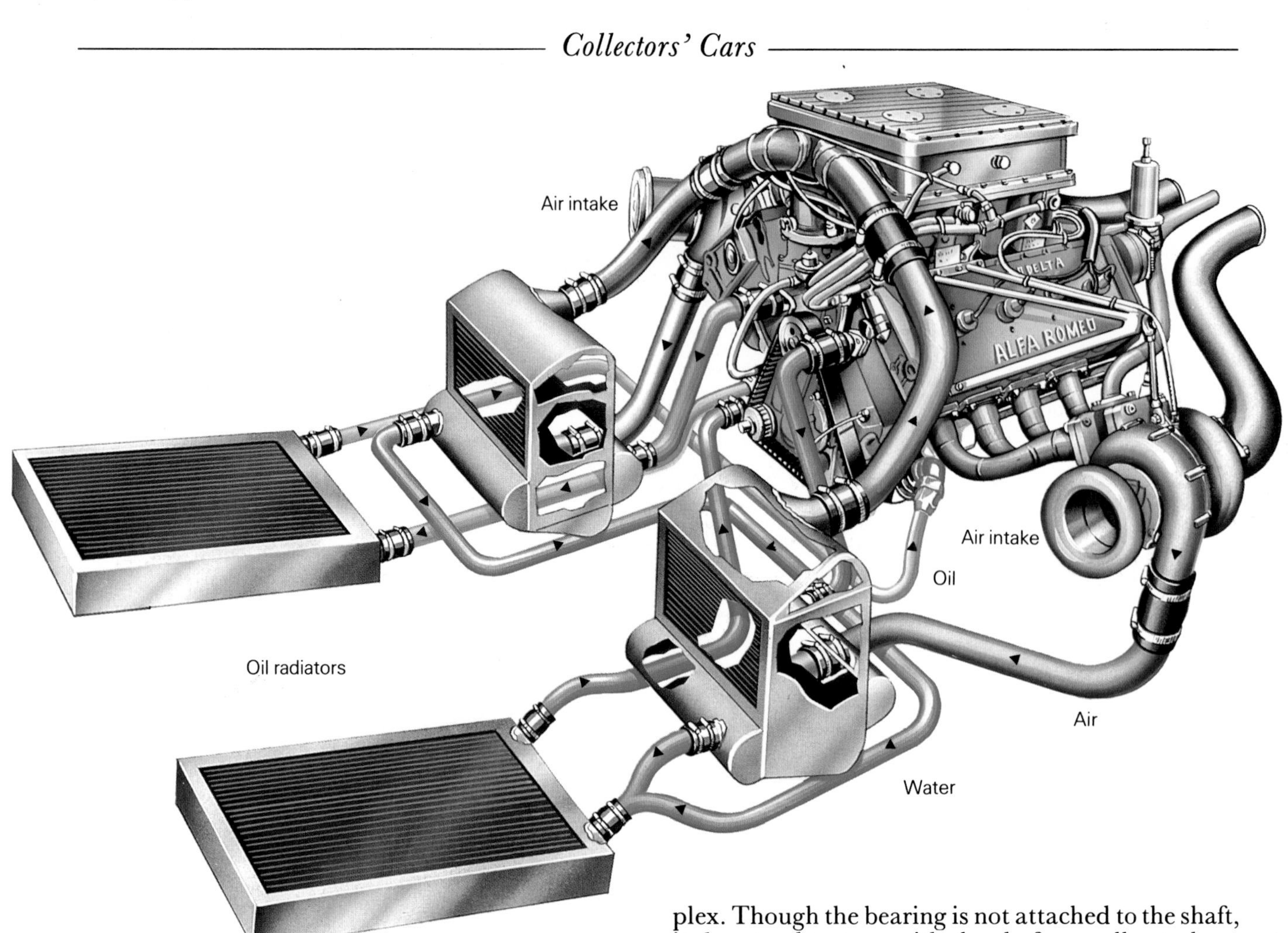

A layout typical of the modern Formula One engines, in this case a twin-turbo Alfa Romeo V8

decided, a turbine has to be designed that will give the required compressor speeds. Turbine design is largely concerned with making the best use of the pulsations that occur in the exhaust when each cylinder fires. So some turbochargers have what amounts to an inlet manifold. The exhaust from the first and fourth cylinders is fed into one part of the turbine housing, and the exhaust from the second and third enters at another. This gives even boost.

All turbochargers employ a centrifugal compressor, whose delivery pressure rises with the square of its speed. This means that, for example, a centrifugal compressor giving 8 psi of boost at 6,250 rpm engine speed would deliver only 2 psi of boost at 2,500 rpm.

Lubrication

Other important features of turbocharger design are the bearings and their lubrication. Most turbochargers are fitted with floating bearings, which support the main shaft between the turbine and the compressor.

Floating bearings fit loosely over the turbine shaft and are also loose inside the turbocharger housing. Oil is fed into the space between the housing and the bearing, and it also reaches the inside of the bearing.

Getting oil to the inside of the housing is straightforward: it is fed directly through a channel in the casing; however, feeding it to the shaft is more complex. Though the bearing is not attached to the shaft, it does tend to turn with the shaft, usually at about half the shaft's speed. A series of holes is therefore drilled in the bearing, and when the bearing turns these act as a pump, drawing oil on to the shaft.

The oil for the turbocharger is taken from the engine's lubrication system, directed over the bearings and returned to the engine. The turbine often rotates at 100,000 rpm, so the efficiency of the system is crucial. Even the briefest interruption in the supply of oil would weld the bearing to the shaft. The oil is also a coolant.

The larger turbochargers require a gallon of oil a minute and the oil returns to the engine looking, in the words of one expert, like 'dirty whipped cream'.

Also associated with the bearings are the seals which isolate the bearings from the turbine and the compressor. The seal between the turbine and the bearings is often a simple ring, rather like a piston ring. This is inserted into a groove in the bearing housing and is made tight enough to stop gas entering. A labyrinth seal is used on some turbochargers, in which the bore of the bearing housing is ridged at the point where the shaft enters, to prevent exhaust gas entering. The seal at the compressor end of the housing is more complicated, consisting of a spring-loaded collar, which bears against the turbine shaft. An O ring completes the seal.

Exhaust system

The final component in a turbocharger installation is the exhaust system and this is in two parts: the manifold before the turbocharger and the piping after it, both components being very durable.

Before it reaches the turbocharger the exhaust gas must retain as much of its heat, speed and pressure as possible in order to keep the turbine spinning efficiently. Consequently, the pipes of the exhaust manifold are relatively narrow and in high-performance cars they will not exceed the diameter of the exhaust pipes. Some American turbocharging enthusiasts even go to the lengths of lagging the early stages of the exhaust pipe to stop the exhaust gases from losing too much heat.

Rather different priorities apply to the section after the turbocharger. Once the gas has been through the turbocharger it is essential to get it out of the system as rapidly as possible, so the gas will not clog up the pipe and restrict the flow of following gas through the turbocharger.

When the exhaust gas emerges from the turbocharger it is spinning and is therefore following a much longer path than is necessary. The piping from the turbocharger often expands abruptly: this breaks down the spinning action of the exhaust gas into a more even flow and accelerates its exit from the pipe.

Turbochargers in use

A turbocharger has three great practical advantages. First, it can produce a great deal of power from a small engine. Second, it does so without adding substantially to the car's weight. A turbocharger does not normally weigh more than 11 kg (25 lb), so a turbocharged 2-litre car can enjoy the acceleration of a heavy 4-litre car, yet retain the superior handling of the light saloon. Third, this performance can be achieved with a comparatively modest fuel consumption, mainly because the turbocharger is driven by a source of power that all other cars waste.

All of these advantages are apparent in, for example, the Saab Turbo, a two-door saloon which has only a 4-cylinder, 2-litre engine, yet performs on equal terms with cars of a superior class. The turbocharger has been designed to give rapid acceleration rather than sheer top speed. It reaches 96 km/h (60 mph) from a standing start in 9.1 seconds, and accelerates from 48 km/h (30 mph) to 80 km/h (50 mph) in 3 seconds. This compares with 9.6 seconds and 3.6 seconds for the Jaguar XJ6, which has an engine more than twice the size of the Saab's. Further, the average petrol consumption is 8.8 km/litre (25 mpg), while the Jaguar manages only 6 km/litre (17 mpg).

These figures have not been achieved by simply bolting the turbocharger straight on to a standard Saab engine. The compression ratio of the engine has been lowered and a low profile camshaft fitted. These modifications help to give the car its rapid acceleration from low speeds and make the car much easier to drive in traffic.

Turbocharging has another incidental benefit. Environmental considerations have had a powerful influence on car design, as anti-pollution laws have forced the development of cleaner engines. Turbochargers tend to lessen exhaust emissions, because the compressor gives better fuel mixing and more even distribution within the engine. This results in the reduction of harmful exhaust gases.

Turbochargers in motor racing

The ability of a turbocharger to extract a great deal of power from a relatively small engine has also been exploited in motor racing. Grand Prix regulations allow normal 3-litre engines or 1.5-litre turbocharged units to be fitted, but despite this capacity penalty many teams have brought out turbocharged engines. Initially Renault was the forerunner in this move but now all GP cars are turbocharged. A turbo can produce more power than the extremely successful 3-litre Ford Cosworth DFV engine.

The Blower Bentley which had a 'supercharged' 4.5-litre engine. The supercharger can be seen bolted to the front below the radiator

TRANSMISSION

THE POWER TRAIN

The transmission system takes power from the engine via the fly wheel and feeds it to the driven wheels of the car. On most recent cars it incorporates a clutch, a gearbox (which allows better use to be made of the engine's power), a propeller shaft and a differential, all of which are designed to provide a smooth transfer of power, under any road conditions, to the driven wheels.

The power produced by the engine can be carried through a number of different basic transmission layouts to the driven wheels. A large proportion of cars have the engine mounted at the front of the car and the transmission system conveys the power to the rear wheels. Since the 1960s, however, an increasing number of manufacturers have mounted the engine in the front of the car, with the transmission system designed to transmit the power to the front wheels.

A further system, adopted by some manufacturers in the past but largely discarded by the 1980s, is one which mounts the engine at the back of the car with the transmission system designed to deliver the power to the rear wheels.

The clutch

The clutch is the means through which the power produced by the engine can be used by the driver. Most cars use a clutch which operates on the friction principle. The main component is a friction disc which is splined on to the input shaft of the gearbox so that it turns with the shaft but is free to slide along it. The disc is pressed against the face of the fly-wheel on the rear of the engine by a strong spring and the two surfaces provide a friction link through which the power produced by the engine is transmitted to the gearbox.

When the clutch pedal inside the car is depressed, the two faces come apart and the engine power is prevented from passing to the gearbox. As a consequence, gears can be changed without risk of them 'graunching'. In most cases, the clutch housing is bolted to the engine crankcase and the gearbox casing is either integral with the clutch housing or bolted to it. In the case of the friction clutch, the clutch friction plate slides on the gearbox input shaft and torque is transmitted from the fly-wheel to the disc by means of friction, as previously explained. But, in place of the single spring, several smaller springs are used and these are positioned in a cover which is bolted to the fly-wheel and which rotates with it. The springs do not rest on the friction plate, however, but operate through a pressure plate which slides on pins attached to the cover. This type of design has now been further improved and simplified by the use of a single diaphragm spring to provide the pressure.

The clutch can be operated through a mechanical linkage or hydraulically through a system similar to that used to activate modern braking systems. In the hydraulic system when the clutch pedal is depressed, the piston in the master cylinder moves forward and the fluid in the system is pressurized. This pressure is transmitted through a small bore pipe which links the clutch master cylinder to a slave cylinder mounted at the side of the clutch housing. This

A 1922 Morris Cowley, one of the last cars to have a multi-plate clutch despite the availability of better systems

Introduced in 1966, the Jensen FF had four-wheel drive developed by Ferguson

A 1940 Oldsmobile Hydra-Matic with the first fully automatic transmission system. It had four forward gears and one reverse

pressure causes the slave piston tomove backwards to operate the clutch release lever.

The gearbox

A gearbox is a set of gears or cogs controlled by a shifting lever which provides a selection of gear ratios between two components of any machine. In the case of the automobile it is located in the drive train between the engine and the drive wheels and provides the means by which the low torque produced by the engine at low speeds can be multiplied. Because a great deal of torque is required to move the car from the stationary, the gear ratio between the engine and the driving wheels must be such that the crank-shaft of the engine is turning over at a relatively high speed while the rest of the transmission is turning slowly.

In any gear system, a reduction in speed means an increase in torque or 'twisting force'. Consequently, the gearbox, when first gear is selected, transmits less speed from the small layshaft gear to the large transmission gear (because when two gears turn together the larger gear turns more slowly) but transmits more torque from the crank-shaft to 'twist' the propeller shaft and overcome the inertia of the car when it is stationary to get it moving.

To explain the principles of the automotive gearbox more easily we will use a three-speed box. A three-speed gearbox consists of an input shaft with a clutch gear on it which turns when the clutch is engaged, a layshaft which has four gears on it—one of which is always meshed with the clutch gear and is turned by it—and a transmission shaft which transmits the power to the propeller shaft. This has two gears on it, one larger than the other, splined so that they can slide on the shaft. Each of the two gears on the transmission shaft is fitted with a shifting yoke which is, in fact, a bracket for pushing them back and forth on the shaft. These yokes are selected and shifted by the driver moving the gear lever.

When first gear is selected, the larger of the two gears on the transmission shaft is pushed along the shaft until it meshes with the smallest gear on the layshaft. If the clutch is then engaged, power will be permitted to pass from the engine through the gearbox and the other parts of the transmission system to the drive wheels. The transmission will then be turning much slower than the input shaft but its torque will consequently be higher.

When second gear is selected the small transmission gear is engaged with the large layshaft gear so the speed of the transmission shaft will rise. If third gear is selected the smaller transmission gear is forced against the clutch gear. Both these gears have teeth on the sides of them which engage and have the effect of making the transmission shaft and the input shaft turn at the same speed.

Reverse gear is at the back end of the layshafts and turns a small idler gear which meshes with the larger transmission gear when reverse gear is selected. (When two gears mesh, they turn in opposite directions; therefore, the inclusion of an idler gear between them makes them turn in the same direction, so that the direction of motion of the car is reversed.)

Synchromesh

In the early days of automobiles, gearboxes were simple devices of the kind described above and their

Lithe lines and a sophisticated transmission, this Delahaye from the mid-1930s has a Cotal electro-magnetic gearbox

smooth operation required a great deal of effort, concentration and skill. Consequently, ways of making gearbox operation simpler and easier were devised, the most significant of which being the introduction of synchromesh.

In this system the gears are made to run at the correct speed before they mesh and consequently avoid any risk of 'graunching' the gears. One method of doing this is to provide conical sections on the sides of the gears which fit into one another, friction starting the gear to turn before the teeth actually mesh. In some designs a 'baulking' mechanism is incorporated to make sure that the gears cannot mesh until they are running at speed. An alternative system has all the gears meshing all the time, but power is not transmitted until a sliding 'dog' axially (lengthwise) engages the appropriate gear. All manual gearboxes use sliding dog clutches to engage the gears.

Automatic transmissions

Automatic transmissions are fitted as standard equipment to the majority of North American cars and are available both as standard equipment and optional extras on many cars produced in Europe, Australia and Japan.

By 1940, General Motors had solved all the problems of producing a true, fully-automatic transmission and they launched such a system in their Oldsmobile models using the type name Hydra-Matic. The first Hydra-Matics had four forward speeds and one reverse, using either three or four epicyclic trains and taking the engine drive through a fluid fly-wheel. The control mechanism used hydraulic valves and complex actuators and the same basic principles are used in the control system of most of today's automatic transmissions. The gear change points were determined by the throttle opening and car's speed.

The typical modern automatic transmission differs in three main respects from the Hydra-Matic, though none of them is really fundamental.

No clutch pedal

One of the most significant differences between a car with automatic transmission and a car with a manually-operated gearbox is the fact that the former has no clutch pedal. The drive is transmitted by hydraulic clutch and gear changes are made automatically, the point of change being decided by the speed of the engine and the load placed upon it.

Being freed from the responsibilities of changing gear relieves the driver of a good deal of physical and mental stress, especially in heavy city traffic.

The tiny gear lever of the Cotal-equipped Delahaye encouraged swift gear changes and required the minimum of physical effort

Front-wheel drive

Many transmission systems employ a different lay-out to the clutch—gearbox—propeller shaft—differential design of the 'centre-line' transmission.

The most important departures from the centre-line transmission are found on cars that have front-wheel drive. The Mini, for example, has a transverse engine. This means that the crankshaft runs across the car, rather than along it. The transmission is located in the sump and the gearbox and the final drive are combined. Two gears take the place of the crown wheel and pinion because the transverse engine ensures that no right-angled drive is required in the drive train.

No propeller shaft is used because the drive from the combined transmission unit is transmitted to the wheels by two drive-shafts. As these shafts have to operate on steered wheels and cope with suspension movement, they employ a special type of coupling called a constant velocity joint.

This, however, is not the only form of front-wheel drive as some cars have longitudinally-mounted engines. Many modern cars have a clutch and gear-box on the car's centre-line but the output shaft from the gearbox leads forward under the engine to where the differential is located. Short shafts, of a similar type to the Mini's, then take the drive to the front wheels.

Another variant is to have the fly-wheel and clutch at the front of the engine next to the radiator. A shaft from the clutch goes over the differential into the gearbox and the output shaft from the gearbox is led to the final drive and differential. Drive-shafts then run to the front wheels. This type of transmission is used on some Citroens and certain Renaults. Exactly the same layout is used on some rear-engined cars.

Rear engine transmissions

Rear-engined cars use a further variety of transmission systems. The Chrysler Imp had the gearbox, differential and final drive combined in a compact unit called a trans-axle. The output shaft occupies the position of the layshaft in a normal gearbox and it carries the final drive bevel pinion at its rear end. Power, therfore, enters and leaves the gearbox at the flywheel end; the differential is located just below and forward of the fly-wheel housing. Short drive-shafts and flexible couplings feed the power to the rear wheels of the car.

The 1931 Vauxhall Cadet featured crude but workable synchromesh and was popular with people looking for less strenuous driving

CHASSIS DESIGN

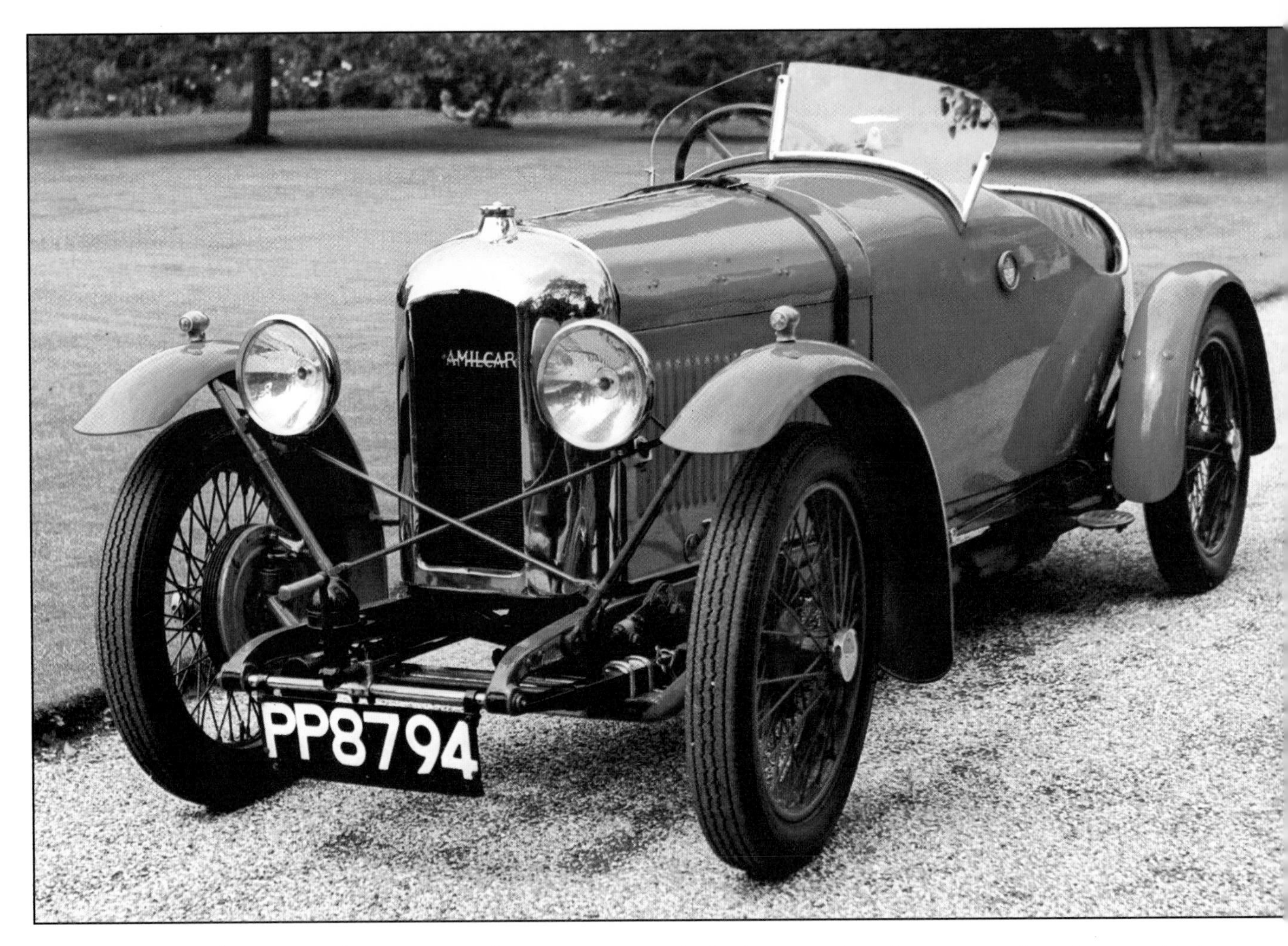

An essential part of any car is some form of under-structure to carry the bodywork, power unit and suspension systems and which will withstand the loadings imposed when the vehicle is at rest or in motion.

Requirements were relatively simple when the first cars were built. Engine power outputs were low and the roads, by present-day standards, were appalling, so speeds on the straight and round corners were very modest. Because of the consequently low dynamic loadings, the primary purposes of the frame were to cope with the weight of the vehicle and the upward reactions from the road.

In effect, the chassis frame had merely to be a beam, loaded downward somewhere near the middle through the centre of gravity of its own structure and the items carried on it, and upward at the ends from the wheels. It followed that the main requirement was 'beam stiffness' or resistance to bending in the vertical plane under these opposing forces which otherwise create handling difficulties.

Early chassis frames

The early chassis frames were therefore designed on what were essentially 'static' principles, but with a margin of strength to deal with road impacts and other dynamic forces which, as indicated above, were not very high. Two straight side members were clearly a good starting point in view of what had to be attached above and below and these longitudinals were bridged by simple cross members. The engine was rigidly mounted, either between the side-members or on cross members and so helped to considerably stiffen the structure.

Since the early 1950s, several distinct paths of chassis development have been followed, simultaneously, by various manufacturers. In order to avoid confusion in this book, however, each path is considered as a whole rather than in a strict chronological order.

In the post-war period there have been only two revolutionary developments in unitary construction;

Vincenzo Lancia with his Lambda model, the car that could have taught the motor industry so much if only it had bothered to listen

both concern materials, not principles. Otherwise, progress in the field of unitary construction has been largely evolutionary, the engineering objectives being to improve the structural efficiency (thus enabling weight to be saved or stiffness to be enhanced or, sometimes, both), refinement and durability. It says much for Citroen's abilities in the 1930s that their original design has undergone no dramatic changes.

Unitary construction

Advances in unitary construction have been shared between the design and production engineers. On the one hand, methods of structural analysis have progressed a long way from the original, almost 'trial-and-error' approach. During recent years, the computer has been increasingly used as a design aid. Its ability to perform complex calculations at great speed has increased the designers' scope. It has also made possible the adoption of the most modern, mathematically-based structural techniques such as 'finite-element analysis' in which the body/chassis unit is broken down into a large number of readily analyzable elements.

In parallel, much has been learned about building unitary structures. Methods of spot welding (used for most joints) are far better than they were and research has shed light on such previous unknowns as the optimum spacing of the spots to achieve the desired integrity. Automation of the welding equipment is another area of major progress and the stage has now been reached where, in a number of big factories, car bodies are built almost entirely by ingenious 'robots' in conjunction with complicated mechanical-handling installations.

A unitary body is more sensitive to corrosion than a hefty separate chassis and many of the first generation of post-war cars—and even the second—used to rust away in vital regions with alarming rapidity. This propensity was accelerated by the growing use of salt on roads to disperse snow or ice in winter, brine being highly corrosive to steel. While paint system inadequacies were partly responsible, designers were also culpable for providing joints with built-in water traps and hollow members without drainage, ventilation and rust-resistant internal treatment.

Fortunately, corrosion protection is another area where, though perfection is still elusive, big improvements have been effected by a variety of means. Not only have the design faults mentioned above been largely eradicated but use is now made of measures such as dip-priming by the electrophoretic process to ensure full penetration of hollow sections, the subsequent internal spraying of these with protective fluids, underbody coating systems and even the employment of zinc-coated steel in the most vulnerable regions. As an indication of what can be achieved by these methods, several models are now guaranteed against structural corrosion for not less than six years.

The tendency of the unitary body to transmit road

Left: *Cars such as this 1927 Amilcar have the chassis side members beneath the rear axle in conjunction with under-slung rear springs*

To lessen body roll, some manufacturers attached semi-elliptic springs below the rear axle rather than in the usual upper position

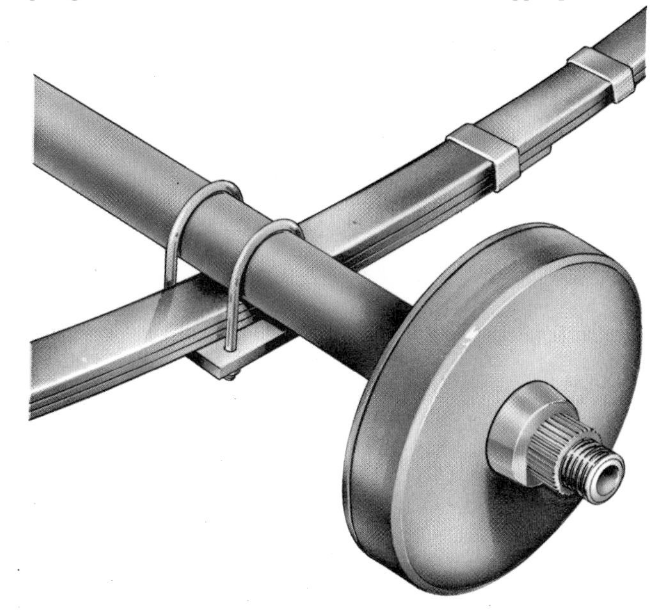

Many cars produced by A.C. between 1954 and 1974 were constructed around a strong tubular ladder-type chassis

and mechanical noise and vibration was the subject of a great deal of research in the late 1950s. An effective solution proved to be carrying the offending items, such as the engine and gearbox and/or the suspension, on a separate subframe attached to the underbody through isolating mountings, usually made of rubber.

Subframes

BMC adopted the subframe concept on Alec Issigonis' Mini in 1959 and then on the 1100 models and it has since been used on many other cars. It has the secondary advantage of facilitating major maintenance work, since the subframe and the components that it carries can be detached relatively quickly as a unit to give much better accessibility. On the debit side, though, the car becomes heavier. More weight goes into the subframe than can be saved in the surrounding main structure since the rubber mountings reduce the former's stiffening effect on the latter. Increasing emphasis on weight reduction, as a fuel-saving means, has caused subframes to lose some of the popularity for small cars. However, they still find favour in Europe for some models in which the weight increase is a lower percentage of the total and the need of refinement is greater.

While the integrity of the full unitary construction is advantageous in most respects, the repair of accident damage becomes expensive should it be necessary to cut out a damaged area and weld in a replacement. To reduce the cost of such repairs it has become quite common practice to relieve the most vulnerable parts—the wing panels—of their structural function, thus enabling them to be separate, bolt-on components which can easily be removed for repair or renewal.

Space and multi-tube frames

One of the earliest space frame chassis was that of Dr Ferdinand Porsche's Cisitalia sports car of 1947. Dr Porsche chose the space frame because of its high ratio of stiffness to weight, a virtue that subsequently led to its adoption for numerous racing cars—Lotus and Mercedes-Benz amongst them—and a few specialist sports cars. Frames of this type are still preferred today for some racing cars in the lower categories of open-wheel formulae.

A true space frame is a three-dimensional structure built from a large number of straight, small-diameter tubes. It has full triangulation in all planes, which means that there are no unbraced quadrilaterals, so in theory every joint could be pinned on without loss of rigidity. In practice, though, the joints between the various tubes (normally of steel) are welded.

Practicalities also force designers to depart—sometimes substantially—from the ideal of full triangulation—in order to install the engine, or to allow the driver to get into the cockpit and feed his legs through one bay of the structure into another. Where transverse triangulation is ruled out, the usual solution is to use a hoop-type bulkhead with sufficient strength to resist 'lozenging'. In some other instances the bracing can be effected, externally, to a particular quadrilateral instead of being situated within it.

The true space frame's high efficiency is matched by high cost, owing to the many man hours required to mitre the tubes and weld the joints. Some specialist-car designers have, therefore, chosen the less efficient multi-tube frame which is cheaper to build than the space frame and is still considerably stiffer in torsion than the ladder variety.

Multi-tube frames are based on four side rails which are tubes of larger diameter than those in a spaceframe design. The distance between the upper and lower pairs of rails is as great as possible, in order to ensure that the frame is as three-dimensional as possible. They are connected by relatively few uprights, with diagonal bracing where feasible. Tubes or hoops form the transverse spacers and bulkheads and in some cases incorporate some triangulation to increase the strength. In some instances the side rails are curved outwards to allow room for seats between them instead of comprising a series of straight lines between cross members. Although such curving is theoretically bad practice, it does not seem to have a serious weakening effect provided the tubes are of sufficiently substantial section.

The Mini Cooper was a highly successful version of Issigonis's Mini, which was outstanding in international rallies and racing

Colin Chapman's first unitary design was the Lotus Elite which features a glass-reinforced plastic (GRP) bodyshell

CHASSIS AND RUNNING GEAR

WHEEL DEVELOPMENT

Ever since the invention of the wheel, which took place in about 3500 BC, people have taken a pride in riding in and on wheeled vehicles. Given fairly round wheels and reasonably smooth paths, the problem of friction in early wheels was concentrated in the fat-greased hub bearing; today, modern hubs run on grease-lubricated rollers inside endless tracks which, in rigid form, is what wheels effectively are.

The primary function of the modern wheel is to transmit the power of the engine in the form of rotary movement from the vehicle to the road; but it also has to support the weight of the car and, as well as coping with the tractive or driven forces, it has to cope with the braking and cornering forces. The design of the wheel is thus extremely important.

The designer has to build into the wheel sufficient strength and stiffness to perform the necessary tasks and, at the same time, ensure that the finished article is sufficiently light so that it affects the ride and handling characteristics of the vehicle as little as possible.

The main requirements of a modern car wheel are that it should be light, strong enough to resist the various forces acting upon it, relatively cheap to produce and easy to clean and remove. In the majority of cases, these requirements are met by a design in which the wheel is bolted directly to the hub, although in some cases the disc or central part of the wheel is permanently joined to the hub and the rim is detachable. In the case of the wire spoke type of wheel fitted to some sports cars, a central nut retains the wheel to the splined hub which mates with internal splines in the centre of the wheel in order to transmit the braking and tractive forces.

The wheel has to be designed to accommodate a tyre on its rim, so the contours are carefully arranged to ensure that when the tyre is inflated it is securely locked on to the wheel; but adequate provision must also be made for the fitting of the tyre, so if the rim is not of the detachable kind, it is necessary to incorporate a well. This allows one side of the tyre to be pressed into the recess, permitting the other side to be levered up and over the opposite rim flange. When the tyre is inflated, air pressure causes the tyre to ride up over the taper at the edge of the rim and thereby 'lock' the beads securely into position on the wheel.

Wheel design became more critical with the advent of new tyres, such as the new generation of low-profile tyres, each of which requires a special wheel to be fitted. As tyre design progresses, so must wheel design—there are now such radical differences between tyres that it is no longer possible, or desirable, to use standard rims as has been normal practice in the past.

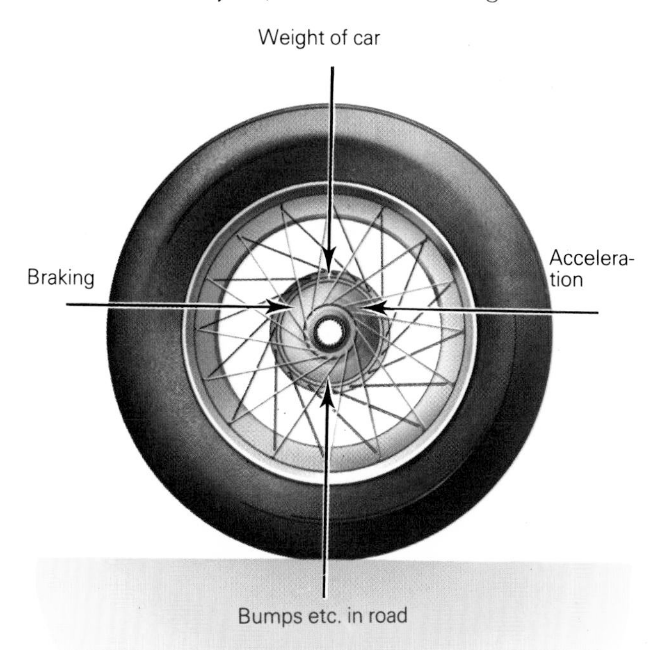

Even under normal driving conditions, wheels have to resist a number of forces acting in a variety of directions

Left: *Wire wheels, as on this Jaguar MkI, were very popular with sporting or performance cars because of their stylish looks*

Below: *A good example of pressed-steel wheels on the early 1950s Standard Vanguard*

The wire-spoked wheel

Since they have little or no resistance to bending stresses, the spokes of a wire wheel have to be laced in a complex pattern achieving triangulation in all three planes to ensure that all the loads put on to the wheel can be resolved into purely tensile ones, shared by sufficient spokes for the purpose.

The spokes are arranged in two or three sets of rows and have four separate, though obviously interconnected, functions to perform. First, they have to take the vertical load or weight of the car; they have to transmit the driving torque between the hub and the rim (and from the rim, the road); similarly, they have to transmit and withstand the braking torque which acts in the opposite direction to the driving torque; and, finally, they have to take all the lateral loads to which the wheel is subjected—particularly when the vehicle is cornering at speed.

Admirable in its structural elegance, the construction of such a wheel is nevertheless labour-intensive and, therefore, an expensive job. In the early days of motoring, when labour was still fairly cheap, this was not much of an objection: the wheel was so much lighter than the alternatives then available and was supposedly so much better in allowing draughts of cooling air to reach the brake drum (this was later realised to be a false supposition) that its disadvantages were largely discounted.

Not all these disadvantages were purely monetary. If only a few spokes were over-tight or slightly loose, the rather flimsy rim would be distorted. If a spoke snapped, its outer end would be free to chafe against the tyre's sidewall and eventually even lacerate the inner tube.

Ettore Bugatti's Type 35 benefited greatly from its aluminium wheels as they helped reduce the car's unsprung weight

Pressed-steel wheels

The standard pressed-steel wheel, however, has one major advantage over all other types; it is cheap to produce. The rim can be rolled from straight steel strip; the centre disc can be stamped in a brace of die-sets. With a little welding and possibly a few rivets the wheel is complete. The construction work is quick and easy but rarely very accurate, so the steel wheel is seldom round and true. Even the stud holes are not always exactly where they should be, though some car manufacturers have improved the concentricity of their wheels by central spigot location, the pioneer being Fiat. Reasonably stiff and light and resistant to accidental damage, however, the steel wheel performs very well considering its ever increasing cost.

The pressed-steel wheel has to be designed with great care. It is weak in the central area where the stresses are exceptionally high around the stud holes. Here, any flat or large-radius section of the disc will suffer fatigue from lateral flexure. It is weak in the region of ventilation holes (which are necessary to cool the brake assembly), unless the edges have been expensively swaged. It is weak again in the area of concentrated stresses where the disc is attached to the rim. Its fatigue life is far from impressive and it is liable to rust. Despite all these potential drawbacks, it is possible to design an efficient pressed-steel wheel, as shown by those fitted to the smaller Citroen cars, but the manufacturing tolerances of steel wheels means that careful and regular balancing will always be necessary.

Light-alloy wheels

A number of modern cars are now fitted with cast light-alloy wheels, either as original equipment or as optional extras and this fashion has much to commend it for it is possible to cast a wheel that is better in every way than the wire wheel, the pressed-steel wheel or any other kind, except the rare and expensive forged light-alloy wheel that has only be seen up to now in racing applications and a few low-volume production models, such as Ferrari road cars on

Bugatti was able to use slim spokes on his type 59 GP car as they did not have to transmit any tractive or braking forces

which excellence is often a higher priority than cost.

Unfortunately, the possibility of universal fitment of light-alloy wheels is seldom realised; to produce the best possible wheel, the unit must be shaped to suit the properties of the cast metal but such shapes are not always those that are the current fashion. Stylists and marketing men prefer flat surfaces, angles and highlights in the wheels, because they look eye-catching in photographs or under showroom lighting conditions, so wheels tend to be designed with corners and edges. Every corner and every angle is a mistake in strict engineering terms because each one is a stress-raiser and an invitation to premature failure.

A badly designed cast light-alloy wheel can thus be dangerous, because the stresses set up within it may eventually result in the wheel failing altogether. A good one, on the other hand is not only lighter than a corresponding steel wheel but is also stronger and more fatigue-resistant and can be machined to close dimensional tolerances that ensure true running—something to which the modern steel-braced radial-ply tyre is very sensitive. Compared with the steel of conventional wheels the aluminium and magnesium alloys are light (or, more accurately, are of lower density) and this permits the use of thicker sections in the critically important areas of the wheel where stresses are set up, enhancing its stiffness and spreading the loads over a wider area to reduce the stress concentrations; the light-alloy wheel thus combines stiffness with a high ratio of strength-to-weight.

Triumph TR7 rally car equipped with tough and sporty Tech-Del Minilite aluminium wheels. Light-alloy wheels are light and strong and therefore excellent for use in competition

One of the best aluminium alloys that is used for the construction of wheels is known as LM25WP, which connotes not only the composition of the alloy but also a long and careful heat process of the finished casting to give it the necessary mechanical properties. Better still, so long as it is treated correctly, is the even lighter magnesium alloy. Normally called Elektron, the magnesium is alloyed with modest quantities of other metals to produce a substance that has a density a quarter that of steel and only two-thirds that of aluminium. For the same weight it is stronger than either; for the strength it is lighter; provided it is correctly made and treated, it also has a longer fatigue life. Its major drawbacks is that it will corrode furiously if brought into contact with salt or as a result of contact with some other metal, such as the steel of a thoughtlessly used wheel nut (aluminium nuts should be employed) or the retaining spring clip of a lead balance weight.

Wheel development

Apart from pressed-steel, wire-spoked and alloy wheels, other wheel designs have been tried. Michelin made—and soon withdrew—a glass-reinforced plastic (GRP) wheel for the Citroen SM. Solid nylon wheels are familiar on go-karts. What comes next may be determined by developments in tyres; new generations of rim profiles, some very shallow, some with humps and hollows of exaggerated profundity, some with wells and some with no wells at all, are currently being promoted to suit some of the most modern tyres. Only one thing seems to be fairly certain; whatever the attractions of any new wheel design, if it cannot be made relatively cheaply it is unlikely to be made at all, at least not in large numbers for the volume car market.

TYRE DEVELOPMENT

Most early tyres were bands of soft iron shrunk around a wooden wheel. Then the development of vulcanised rubber paved the way for the pneumatic tyre, and ultimately the cross-ply and radial.

It was Charles Goodyear who made the discovery accidently, in January 1839, when he dropped part of a mixture of rubber, sulphur and white lead on to a hot stove. The charred lump that he recovered remained flexible when cool and, despite repeated stretching, would always snap smartly back to its original shape. An example was brought over to England and shown to Hancock who, without knowing how Goodyear had achieved his particular result, applied himself to exactly the same problem and came to precisely the same answer.

Now that rubber could be lasticated and generally made to behave itself, it could be applied to carriage wheels, and solid rubber tyres rapidly became popular.

Pneumatic tyre development

By the 1890s the pneumatic tyre had developed, in broad theoretical principles, the features by which it is recognizable today: a tread composed of rubber compounded and vulcanized to resist the abrading action of the road and to afford a suitably secure grip on it, aided by some patterning to suit loose or wet surfaces; beads of steel wire making the mounting of the tyre easy and its displacement from the rim during normal use difficult; textile fabrics to withstand the fatigue of continued flexing and a valve to facilitate inflation. The new tyre was quickly adopted for the motor cars and motor cycles that were beginning to proliferate and very soon the new tyre was also being applied to aircraft, heavy transport vehicles and later to buses, agricultural implements and even railway carriages.

Not all of these developments occurred simultaneously. In particular, the wired-edge tyre seated in a well-based rim took a long time to achieve popularity, only enjoying general acceptance after about 1920. Prior to that decade, all sorts of crude and semi-mechanical arrangements were made for retaining the tyre on the wheel and retaining the air within the tyre, the most lasting of which methods was the beaded-edge tyre; it was, however, as much materials technology as anything else which prevented these developments from occurring at an earlier date.

During the Second World War some experimentation with synthetic rubber was carried out but by

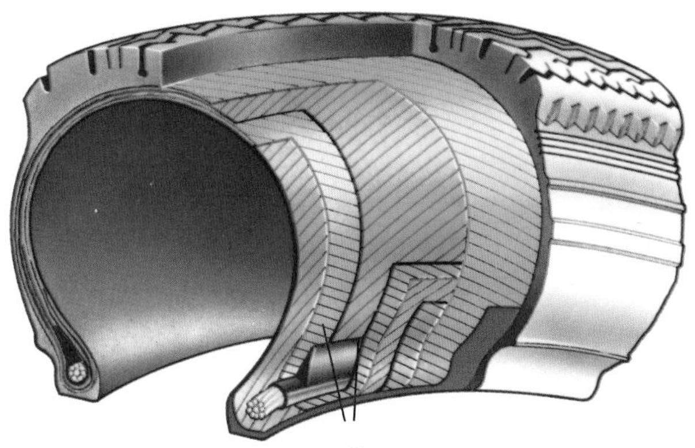

The conventional cross-ply tyre is composed of several textile carcass plies set at opposing angles to each other and at approximately 38 degrees to the centre of the tyre line (crown angle)

Left: *In the early days of motoring, punctures were rife and replacing the tyre or inner tube was strenuous and time-consuming*

1945, the development of synthetics lost its impetus. Cheap natural rubber was again available and it was not until 1948 that the next major breakthrough occurred. This was a curiously constructed tyre that was produced by Michelin. It followed a design pattern that had been used during the war for heavy bombers' tyres by Dunlop; that pattern itself being a development of an idea tried in the Sahara Desert in 1936 by Michelin, and based on a British patent that was granted as early as 1913.

Michelin's tyre was called the radial, after the manner of it construction and was to have a profound effect on tyre design throughout the world. There is little doubt that the first radial tyres were quite revolutionary when introduced to the public; both in terms of behaviour and longevity the new tyres were superior to the existing bias-ply offerings.

For the first 60 years of pneumatics, the tyre industry had never been able to reconcile all of the elements in the long list of daunting requirements mentioned above, every single one of which was incompatible with at least one of the others. Good ride quality could only be achieved at the expense of handling response; wet grip and squeal-free cornering were at odds with long life and low rolling resistance; each aspect of a tyre's required quantities had to be compromised, because the structure of the familiar bias-ply (cross-ply) tyre was one in which every part of the tyre depended on every other part.

This was not true of the radial-ply tyre, in which, for the first time, the principle of 'decoupling' could be exploited; this means that the tread could be designed to function as a tread should, while the sidewalls could be designed to fulfil the necessary requirements of sidewalls, being made in a different way and perhaps of different materials, with the whole structure being divided in a manner that allowed this functional independence.

Eventually, with increasing experience and manufacturing skills, the tyre manufacturers could design each part of the tyre from bead to bead to fulfil its necessary requirements quite independently of each other part of the structure.

The radial arrives

The first such tyres to display this promise came on the market in the late 1940s. They were made by Michelin and while debate raged about whether they should be called belted, rigid-breaker, or radial-ply tyres, what did become well-known was the trade name of 'Michelin X'. Such was the success of the tyre that many believed that Michelin invented the radial-ply tyre, which was no more true than that Dunlop had invented the pneumatic tyre. In fact, the invention can be traced back at least as far as a British patent granted in 1913 to Messrs. Gray and Sloper. They summarized their idea by saying that: 'The tyre cover comprises in combination radially disposed flexible inextensible cords which constitute the sole restraining means at the sides of the tyre, and a girder belt of flexible material inextensible in directions oblique to the circumferential direction of the tyre.' They suggested that the belt might be made of

Auto Union Grand Prix car of the 1930s, when radical car designs forged ahead of tyre development. Cars of this era had a terrific appetite for tyres; pit stops for new tyres were frequent with the main problems being thrown treads or completely shredded rubber

any material that was flexible, but would not stretch; they even suggested as possible areas for development 'straight-thread fabric, canvas, wire or a mixture of these in one or more layers.'

Construction of the radial

Steel wire was the material chosen by Michelin for their X, in recognition of the arduous duties that the belt had to perform. The belt had to be stiff like a girder in every direction except perpendicular to its surface. It had to be resistant to stretch circumferentially, to compression laterally and hence to any kind of distortion obliquely, while remaining pliable enough to manage easily the transition from its natural curvature to a flatness in the contact area or even to a reverse curvature necessary when running over a ridge or stone or some other kind of obstruction on the road's surface.

To achieve this, the belt has to be made in at least two layers of cords which are not truly circumferential but slightly oblique; the angle by which the cords diverge from the circumferential is usually between 18 and 22 degrees and with one layer sloping in one direction and the other in the opposite, the lateral stiffness can be satisfactorily and consistently obtained.

Given a belt of adequate properties, it becomes feasible to resort to the other essential feature of the construction, which is to run the carcass cords radially from bead to bead, crossing the crown of the tyre at right angles, not diagonally. Where they pass under the belt they complete a ring of triangulation with the belt cords that provides the final constraint necessary for control of the tread area; in the sidewalls they remain free to flex considerably, giving great pliability. This freedom to flex provided a very important feature, not only ensuring ride comfort but also in allowing the tyre to remain cool even at high speeds, because the internal friction of such a construction was much less than with the trellising motion of the biased cords in the cross-ply tyre which made it much more a prey to heat build up.

At the same time the radial pliability of the belt and its stiffness in other directions allowed the tread rubber to do just what was required of it, to roll over the ground like the endless tread of a track-laying vehicle such as a tank or bulldozer. The belt's resistance to distortion in other directions prevented the tread from being laterally compressed, as it was in the contact area of the cross-ply tyre, and so reduced the amount of tread distortion which had increased the frictional losses of the cross-ply tyre as well as accelerating its rate of wear.

The result was that the radial-ply tyre was longer lasting, consumed less energy, gave a better ride, especially at higher speed, and superior roadholding. Compared with the old cross-ply alternative, the radial-ply tyre also offered comparative freedom

The Michelin X represented a breakthrough in tyre design in which the belt plies under the tread were set at oblique angles to the crown, while the carcass cords ran radially from bead to bead

Brabham mechanics during a quick tyre change to Ricardo Patrese's car in a 1983 Formula One race. Tyres are changed during races to replace worn rubber

from wander induced by longitudinal ridges in the road surface and from side loadings induced by wheel camber—an apparently obscure advantage that was in fact tremendously important in making acceptable a number of inexpensive forms of independent suspension that had previously been thought unsatisfactory.

However, together with the advantages of the radial-ply tyre came disadvantages which included a harsher low-speed ride, heavier steering at low speeds and when parking, and some handling problems which threatened to make a radial-shod car dangerous to drive.

Another area of development in tyres has been for rallying, where the recent trend has been for top teams to use tyres suited for a wide range of conditions (this is a Fiat 131 Abarth in a forest stage)

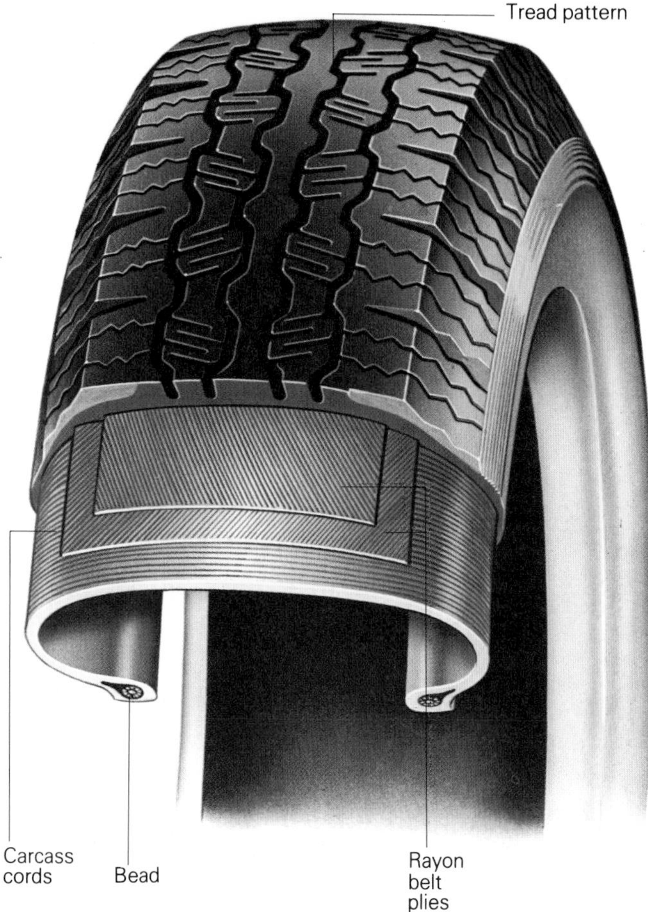

The improvement in radial-ply design of the first Pirelli Cinturato lay in its Rayon cords and belts which made its handling qualities far less unpredictable than those of the earlier Michelin X

Roadholding

When the limit of a cross-ply tyre's cornering power is reached and exceeded, the driver finds that the grip and cornering power progressively deteriorates; thus he can make the necessary steering and throttle corrections before all control is lost and the car spins. However, when the higher limit of cornering power of one of the earlier radial-ply tyres was exceeded, loss of grip was immediate, leaving the driver very little time in which to correct the situation, making a spin almost inevitable for all but the very best drivers. The problem was caused mainly by the compliance of the sidewalls of the tyre and their capacity for considerable lateral distortion.

The first successful answer to this problem was found by Pirelli, who, late in the 1950s produced a radial-ply tyre in which the belts (like the sidewalls) were made of rayon but in a greater number of plies; both the sidewall and the breaker (or belt) plies were formed and laid in ways that ensured a better communication between the two elements without seriously interfering with their independent efficiencies. Thus began the evolution of a new generation of radial-ply tyres in which the real or apparent stiffness of the sidewalls could be increased to improve lateral response and in which a wider range of materials could be exploited—not only in the carcass but also in the rubber—to give almost any desired combination of properties.

SUSPENSION VARIATIONS

Only the various forms of the leaf spring are capable of serving both functions of a suspension system, providing not only the elastic cushioning of the body of the car from the irregularities of the road surface but also the necessary positive linkage between the body and the wheels.

However, the leaf spring does not accomplish this secondary task with as much precision as is desirable; so, despite the greater expense of providing separate means of springing and of axle or wheel location, most manufacturers have recognized the need for doing so. Some of their solutions are evidently cost-conscious; a few, appropriate to the priorities of design in cars of high performance, are costly, both in terms of construction and of the space that is occupied; but most represent some sort of compromise between the two and in certain modern designs this compromise has been effected with remarkable success.

It was the desire to provide for independent movement of the wheels that prompted the development of these suspension linkages when designers grew dissatisfied with the simple beam axles that had served almost all cars quite well for the first few decades of motoring. By the 1930s, car buyers were demanding more comfort and, in some cases, better handling to match the increased performance that was partly due to improvements in engine power. Front wheel brakes were growing in size and weight, as were tyres and wheels, and the relatively soft springs that maintained adequate control of a light beam axle in earlier days could no longer cope. Independent suspension not only halved unsprung mass at a stroke, it also dealt with the rather more involved problem of gyroscopic precessions.

Lateral tilt of a wheel as it rode a bump would induce a turning of that wheel about its steering axis, either to the left or the right, because the wheel acted as a gyroscope: on a beam axle, lateral tilt prompted both wheels to precess in the same direction, making the steering kick viciously, but with independent front suspension (IFS) such precessions would in many cases counter one another. IFS was a more inviting cure than simply stiffening the springs to reduce wheel travel; moreover, it liberated space at the front of the chassis so that the engine could be carried further forward, whether to increase the car's polar moment of inertia, to give more passenger

A sliding-pillar front suspension system, first used on the early three-wheeler Morgans, is still retained on the Morgan Plus 8

A 1929 Lagonda showing the Marles steering box, drag link, track rod, gaitered left spring and anti tramp rod that helped stop the axle from twisting

Dante Giacosa, in the 1930s. What Earle MacPherson did was to simplify and cheapen the mechanism by setting an anti-roll torsion bar in front, bending back the ends so that they could attach to the outer ends of the transverse links and thus provide the necessary triangulation, together with a little longitudinal compliance (by mounting the bar in rubber) to help the radial-ply tyres. The system was relatively inexpensive to produce, accepted loads without problems (though there was a tendency for the struts to bind because of slight bending loads) and fed its loads into the car body at widely separated points, just as the engineers who calculated the various stresses believed correct.

One or two designers experienced problems in strengthening their creation's wheel arches to hold the struts firmly but this was a matter that could easily be solved. Geometrically, the strut system was quite adaptable: camber and other changes could be modulated by varying the angle of the strut away from the vertical and of the transverse link from the horizontal. It was even found possible to tilt the strut

The 1935 Derby Maserati, a one-off Maserati-engined racing car, showing its transverse leaf suspension and front wheel drive. Transverse leaf independent suspension was popular for many years

space or to enable the whole car to be shorter and therefore less expensive to manufacture.

The Lancia Aurelia had double-wishbone IFS and this was the kind that really popularized IFS when the American motor industry adopted it. General Motors debated only two kinds of design—double-wishbones and Dubonnet—but hesitated only briefly before choosing the former. Dubonnet's system featured a steered swinging arm, giving very low unsprung weight with the spring and steering linkage being chassis-mounted but it entailed rather unwelcome variations in steering trail unless the amplitude of wheel movement was severely restricted. This system did not meet GM concepts of ride comfort for their production cars, though Chevrolet and Pontiac first appeared with Dubonnet suspension at the New York Show in November 1934. The other GM divisions adopted wishbones as the basic element of the front suspension and soon Chevrolet and Pontiac fell into line. It was the American endorsement of wishbone IFS that made it statistically by far the most important form of IFS of all time simply because of the size of the American market.

MacPherson strut IFS

Eventually it was another system that most strongly threatened the dominance of wishbones. The British Fords of 1951 introduced the MacPherson strut IFS and this is still the favourite system outside the USA. A telescopic strut with an integral hydraulic damper and (usually) a co-axial helical coil spring carries a stub axle at its bottom, is flexibly mounted to the car body at the top and is located laterally by a transverse link pivoted at its base. If that link is triangulated to give longitudinal location and accept braking forces, a simple strut suspension results, such as had been envisaged by Fiat's gifted designer,

backwards slightly to soften the ride, imitating a backwards tilt of wishbone pivots that had been popular for the same reason. Offset springs and Teflon sliders reduced the binding tendencies and there were no other serious snags, just the enormous advantages of inexpensive construction and very economical use of space.

This lack of clutter made strut suspension particularly suitable for the many new small front-wheel drive cars that proliferated from the 1960s; the spaces liberated by the strut and link afforded ample scope for the articulation of a drive-shaft. At the same time, the growing popularity of front wheel

The good roadholding of the GM Opel Kadett is due in part to a transverse beam and torsion bar connecting the rear trailing arms

drive created new opportunities for rear suspension design, now that it was no longer burdened by the heavy and space-consuming final drive.

The De Dion rear axle

If precise control of the axle's path can be assured, there is much to be said in favour of a beam axle at the rear of a car, with the proviso that if the rear wheels are driven then the transmission should be independent of the suspension. This can be contrived by a splendid compromise known as the De Dion axle, invented by Trepardoux when he was a partner of Georges Bouton and the Marquis Albert De Dion in the 19th century. A 'dead' beam axle of conveniently light tubing carries two wheels and is, itself, carried by springs or any chosen number of links, while the final drive is housed in a chassis-mounted unit connected to the rear wheels by universally-jointed drive-shafts. The brakes can be mounted at the inboard ends of these drive-shafts to reduce the unsprung weight further. As for axle location, this can be as precise as the designer wishes in theory but, in practice, most designers have fallen a long way short of the ideal, usually through their failure to pivot the longitudinal links on the car's centre line. Failing this there will be some spurious rear-wheel steering and the axle beam will, in all probability, act as the equivalent to an extremely stiff anti-roll bar.

Probably the only perfect De Dion axle to go into production, albeit on a limited basis, was that fitted to the Spanish Pegaso vehicle which was the work of Wilfredo Ricart who had earlier designed a similar layout for an unfledged Alfa Romeo racing car. The torsion bar effect could be avoided by putting a sleeve joint in mid-beam, as was first done in the 1937 Mercedes-Benz Grand Prix car; Rover went further in their 1963 P6 2000 model by allowing some telescoping movement in the sleeve, because this avoided the need for splined or otherwise telescoping drive-shafts which tend to bind when subjected to heavy tractive torque. Indeed, the De Dion axle of the Rover was one of the best of its kind, the design being as full of merit as it was of interest.

Rack and pinion steering system of the Lotus Elan, with its double wishbone front suspension, allied to a backbone chassis, and coil-sprung independent rear suspension gave superior roadholding

Rear suspension variations

The idea of using inextensible jointed drive shafts as locating members for the hubs or wheel carriers and thus as part of the rear suspension, was one of those strokes of genius emanating from Colin Chapman. He first used the layout in the rear suspension of the Lotus 18 racing car, although the first steps in this

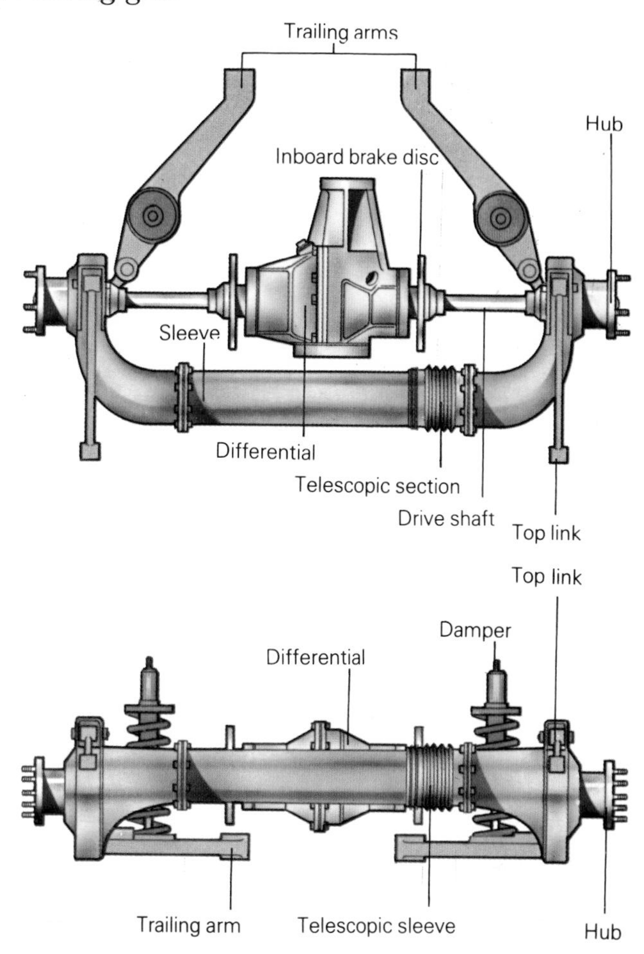

The De Dion rear axle, fitted to a Rover P6, allows telescopic movement in the sleeve to avoid the need for splined drive-shafts

direction were taken as early as 1951 in the Kieft 500 cc/31 cu in racing car. Later, in the 1960s, Jaguar used such shafts in much the same manner as Lotus, making them serve in lieu of the upper elements of a four-bar wishbone type of linkage.

The Kieft had universal joints only at the inboard ends of its drive shafts, being a swing-axle design. The swinging half axle was propounded by Rumpler and Ledwinka in the early 1920s, when chassis dynamics were scarcely understood and Maurice Olley's classic investigations of understeer and oversteer had yet to be started. On the notoriously rough and markedly cambered roads of the Tatra mountains, it seemed to work well, certainly better then contemporary live axles and it provided a particularly inexpensive and easy means of integrating the suspension and the transmission with a rear-mounted engine. Therefore, it was strongly advocated by Porsche for cars as dissimilar as the Volkswagen and the Auto Union, its only virtue in the latter application (as in sundry other over-powered competition cars of the period) being to leave the suspension free from tractive torque reaction and the unsprung mass of the final drive.

The design's greatest vice was its dreadful geometry, creating violent camber changes and a treacherous jacking-up of the rear of the car when cornering, so that the outer wheel could tuck under and lose virtually all its cornering power in a sudden and often disastrous manner.

Strut-type IRS is almost as economical of space and has been used occasionally with the greatest elegance by Fiat whose engineer Cordiano devised a system in which track rods, pivoted to the chassis/body at their inboard ends, applied a carefully calculated steering correction to the orientation of the wheels as they moved up and down, ensuring the best possible behaviour at all times. The Cordiano strut system has proved itself in the Fiat rally cars, the 124 Spyder and the 131 Abarth, as well as in the superb 130 and Dino 2.4 luxury cars which featured such high performance and impeccable roadholding.

Mounted directly onto the suspension, the high-mounted wings presented many problems. After two accidents involving Brabhams at the 1968 Spanish Grand Prix, the wings were quickly banned.

BRAKE - DISC OR DRUM?

Since the early days of motoring the performance of cars has continuously improved, and their braking systems have, therefore, benefitted from a vast amount of technological development in order to keep them in line with the increasing demands of both the driver and the vehicle.

The internal-expanding drum brake was introduced in the early 1900s and soon became the standard form of retardation for road vehicles of all kinds, superseding the external-contracting band brake and other more primitive stopping devices. Its great initial advantages were that, since the friction surfaces were almost completely enclosed, efficiency was not seriously impaired in wet weather and grit could less readily reach the surfaces and cause scoring and consequent rapid wear.

In essence, a typical drum brake comprises the drum itself, normally manufactured from cast iron because of its relatively low cost and good wear properties, a back plate, two shoes faced with friction material and an actuating and release system. The drum revolves with the car's road wheel and its working surface is of cylindrical form, embracing the shoes which are mounted on the stationary backplate; since the latter reacts against the braking forces it has to be rigidly attached to the axle or suspension linkage that carries the road wheel.

Each shoe is pivoted at one end and the actuating force is applied at the other. When the brake is in the 'off' position, the shoes are held clear of the drums by tension return springs. There are usually two of these and they are hooked between the shoes. Application of the brakes causes the shoes to be pivoted outwards, against the resistance of the springs, into contact with the drum where they exert their force.

Expansion of the shoes was effected mechanically until the advent of hydraulic actuating systems in the 1920s and 1930s; initially, mechanical operation was achieved by interposing an elliptical or an arena-shaped cam between the free ends of the shoes. The cam was carried on a spindle supported in the backplate and an external lever on the spindle enabled the latter to be rotated to push the ends of the brake shoes apart.

A rival to this arrangement appeared in the 1930s for those cars that were still fitted with mechanically-operated brakes. It was a Girling development in which the rotating cam was replaced by a transverse wedge on a spindle which was pulled axially by the actuating system. The wedge bore against the tapered ends of the shoes either directly or through rollers, which had the advantage of reducing friction. This mechanism was not only claimed to be more efficient than cam actuation but also equalized the leverage exerted on the two shoes; because the outer end of a cam is working at a larger radius from the

The prototype Rolls-Royce Silver Ghost which like its contemporaries had a braking system that only worked on the rear wheels

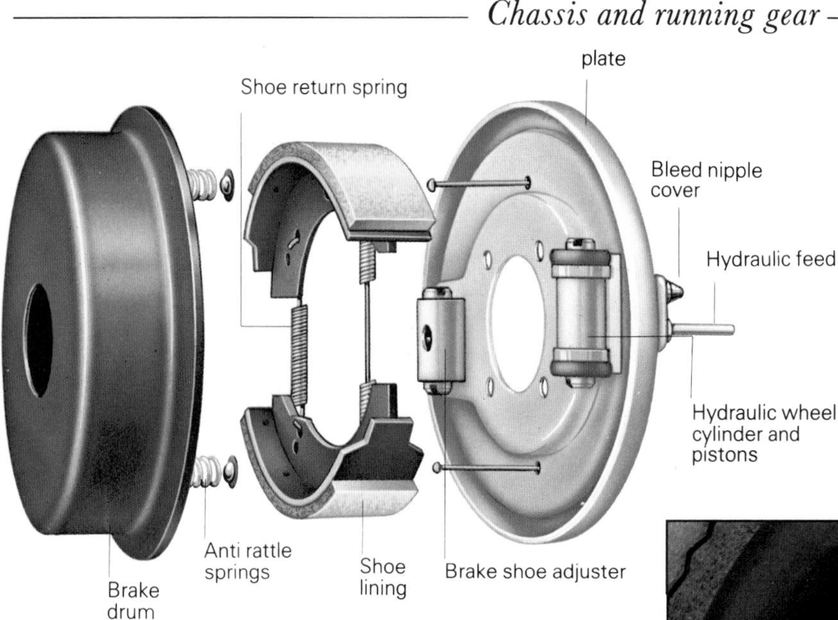

In a typical drum brake, an hydraulic wheel cylinder is fitted to a back-plate, which, in turn, is rigidly attached to the axle or suspension assembly. Hydraulic pressure from the master cylinder moves the wheel cylinder pistons outwards, pressing friction linings against the brake drum which revolves with the road wheel

Trying to overcome brake fade, Mercedes-Benz designed these finned drums in 1937 to increase airflow on their Grand Prix brakes

pivot than the inner end, the shoe it actuates does more of the work.

Twin leading shoes

As the performance of cars increased in the period after the Second World War, it became necessary to improve their stopping abilities. In earlier days this could be done fairly easily by fitting larger brakes which had a correspondingly greater leverage. However, a tendency had arisen for wheel sizes to be reduced as tyre sections became wider, so there was little room for larger-diameter drums to be accommodated within the wheel. A further problem was the extra weight of larger drums and the effect they would have on ride and handling qualities.

One answer to this problem was the introduction of the twin-leading-shoe (2LS) brake. It had long been appreciated that the leading shoe of a leading-and-trailing pair was the more effective of the two. This is because rotation of the wheel tends to pull a leading shoe on to the drum, giving a 'self-servo' or 'self-wrapping' action; in contrast, a trailing shoe tends to be thrown off the drum by wheel rotation. For orthodox 2LS operation, the fulcrums of the shoes are diametrically opposite and each shoe has its own actuating cylinder fed by a divided hydraulic line.

For safety reasons, conventional uni-directional 2LS brakes were not fitted to all four wheels of a car. Their use was confined to the front wheels which, being the more heavily loaded due to weight transfer on deceleration, could take the greater retarding efficiency without locking readily. The rear brakes remained of the leading and trailing type, giving the car reasonable braking during reversing while ensuring that the parking brake—which normally operated on the rear wheels—was equally effective whether the car was pointing up or down a gradient.

The disc brake

The first post-war manifestation of interest in alternatives to the automotive drum brake occurred in the USA—rather surprisingly in view of the limited demands made on brakes by American road-driving conditions. In 1950 the big Chrysler Corporation announced a very different design of disc brake. This sprang from aircraft technology which was then heavily influenced by such brakes because of the vast amounts of heat generated in retarding—even quite gently—the latest big aircraft which had high landing speeds. The Chrysler brake was an enclosed one, almost an inside-out variation since it comprised a double-sided and heavily finned drum containing twin friction discs which were expanded against the sides by a self-energizing ball-and-ramp mechanism similar to that evolved by Girling.

In the early 1950s, the automotive disc brake's gestation period came to an end. Dunlop was one of the companies involved in aircraft braking developments and, being in close touch with the motor racing world through their tyre division, were well aware of the increasing problems facing the drum brake makers. However, aircraft brakes almost invariably had axially-floating discs which were excellent in their own context since braking was done principally in a straight line but under cornering conditions, this configuration was bound to give rise to phenomena such as 'pad knock-off' which could lead to brief delays before the brake became effective on its next application.

Disc brakes for racing cars

Dunlop built prototypes with hydraulic actuation, one appearing on the Dunlop stand at the 1951 London Motor Show, where it attracted a great deal of interest. Intensive testing confirmed Dunlop's hopes and intentions, and Jaguar's Bill Heynes conveyed his enthusiasm so effectively to Sir William Lyons (the founder of Jaguar cars) that one of the works-supported C types was equipped with Dunlop discs for the 1952 Rheims sports-car race. As a result of their promise in this race it was decided that the new brakes should be specified for the following year's Le Mans cars—a decision that Jaguar certainly had no cause to regret.

The C type's success on the Sarthe circuit that year tends to blind people to the fact that Girling, under the leadership of Chief Engineer Arthur Goddard, had been working on similar lines to Dunlop in the early 1950s, their version of the spot brake having actually replaced the drum type on the later versions of the Mk I 1.5-litre supercharged BRM V16 in 1952. At that time, though, BRM was not a race winner for other reasons, so the brakes tended to receive little publicity. This was unfortunate for Girling but it did not discourage them from pressing on, and they eventually took over Dunlop's disc brake activity altogether in 1965.

The disc brake and the road car

By the mid-1950s, when many competition cars were using disc brakes, the manufacturers of high-performance road cars began to demand that their vehicles should be similarly equipped. Thus in 1953 the Triumph TR3 appeared with Girling discs on its front wheels while the Jensen 541 used Dunlop units on all four wheels; in both cases the discs were fitted as standard equipment. Jaguar introduced the Dunlop design as an optional extra on all wheels of some of their models. On the continent, Citroën introduced disc brakes of their own design on the DS19 to maintain their reputation as technological innovators.

Inevitably, Britain's oldest-established brake specialist, Lockheed, could not defer becoming part of the disc brake revolution, and Chief Engineer Leslie Chouings and his team worked hard with J. F. Bradbury on the research and development side to recover the ground lost to Dunlop and Girling. Consequently they were able to participate fully in the next chapter of the story—the move down-market. This progressed through the middle register during the next few years and reached the popular-priced category in 1962 when the year's outstanding newcomers—the Issigonis-designed BMC 1100 and the Ford Cortina—appeared with front disc brakes from Lockheed and Girling respectively.

On other than light cars, the solution had to be to boost the hydraulic pressure by means of a vacuum servo. The 1960s therefore saw a proliferation of such servos, tailored to the requirements of the new brake systems. Initially, following existing practice, the servo was a separate item but before long cost and weight were being saved by integrating it with the master cylinder for direct actuation from the pedal.

Automatic adjustment

Another problem that had to be overcome at an early stage was that of adjustment. Since disc brake pads are relatively small, to minimize shrouding of the disc from the airflow, they have to be thick for adequate life; pedal or handbrake-lever travel therefore tends to increase considerably as the pads become worn. The consequent need for automatic adjustment was met in several ways, the most elegant (and subsequently the most widely used) being Dunlop's special sealing ring which normally served to retract the pad from the disc on release of the pedal but slipped slightly to take up a new datum position when pedal travel became excessive. With 'mixed' disc/drum systems, the incorporation of automatic adjustment at the front soon brought a

When introduced in May 1955, the D-type Jaguar was the first European production car to be fitted as standard with disc brakes, following the success of the C-type at Le Mans in 1953

Above: *George Eyston's Thunderbolt Land Speed Record car that used an early hydraulic disc braking system*

Below: *The GM Nash of 1938 had drum brake cooling problems because of enclosed wheels and enveloping wings*

demand for matching automaticity at the rear, and the Ford Cortina's Girling equipment was one of the first to feature this double-ended approach.

All three British suppliers (and their imitators elsewhere) originally used fixed, double-acting calipers having piston-actuated pads on both sides, with cross-connection to balance the clamping forces. However, the down-market move at the beginning of the 1960s forced designers to reduce costs through simplification and weight saving. Their efforts led to a variety of swinging or sliding calipers with an inboard cylinder only—a layout pioneered by Crosley in their 1948 brake.

Probably the most significant recent innovation has been the initiation of a swing from asbestos-based to other friction materials for the pads, including carbon fibre. Not yet certain is the form that non-asbestos materials will take in the longer term, since there are two main avenues of progress. Ferodo worked, for ordinary road cars, on other varieties of fibre although still feeling that asbestos had the best all-round balance of properties. Other makers concentrated on the more costly sintered metallic or ceramic/metallic materials which first featured in clutches and brakes in heavy earth-moving equipment; such materials are already in limited service in arduous car disc brake applications where their excellent thermal stability is extremely valuable.

STEERING

The early years of steering development undoubtedly took place during an inopportune period of motor history. Most roads were little more than cart tracks, and to steer a car along paths of such diverse contours was a practice fraught with difficulties.

It is doubtful whether anyone ever thought that improving the steering system's design would lead to any increase in the ease of controlling the cart, carriage or early and somewhat eccentric car. However, as time moved on the advances made in all forms of technology accelerated with astonishing rapidity, things began to improve.

With the introduction of independent front suspension a simple track rod connecting the wheels was no longer suitable because of the track changes that occurred as the wheels moved up and down. Designers found it necessary to go over to two-piece and even three-piece track rods, with a slave lever, to keep the wheel correctly aligned on other than smooth roads.

Rack and Pinion

On the credit side, the advent of independent front suspension meant that the movement of the axle relative to the link was tamed, thus removing a major objection to rack-and-pinion steering; the other objection of excessive road reactions at the steering wheel had already been greatly reduced by the big improvement in road surfaces and the increase in tyre sections. In fact, the reversibility of the gearing

As more demands were made on the steering system, the worm-and-sector design was developed to reduce violent kickback

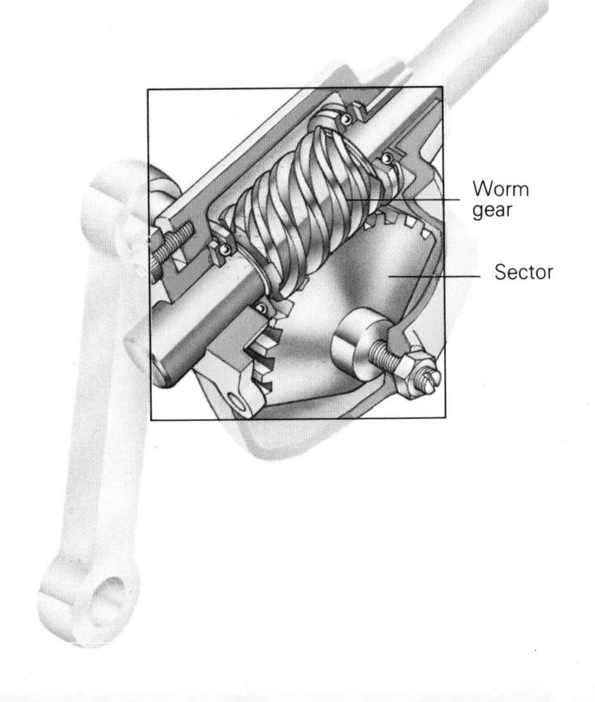

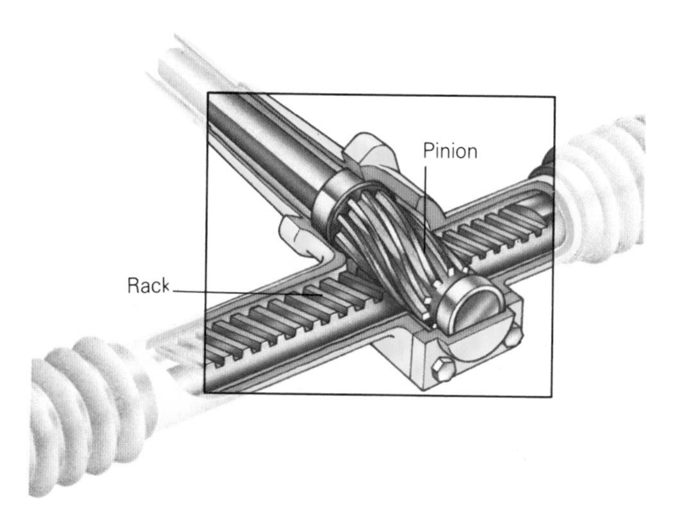

Though acceptable, worm gearing was unnecessarily complex so some designers opted for the simpler rack-and-pinion system

Left: *Probably the first cars to use rack-and-pinion steering were Adler's Trumpf models of 1932. This is the 1938 Trumpf Junior*

could now be turned to advantage since it gave the steering a sensitivity that kept the driver informed of what was happening at the front wheels.

Adler in Germany appear to have been the first to take up rack-and-pinion steering for cars with independent front suspension—in their Trumpf and Trumpf Junior front-drive models of 1932. Then, after a year or two of production of the revolutionary Traction Avant (introduced in 1934), André Citroën went over to rack-and-pinion, thereby bringing the steering to the same high standard as the ride and roadholding. Then, in the early post-war years, Alec Issigonis made his mark as a production car designer with the Morris Minor—one of the most-loved models ever. Not the least contributor to its charm was its light and precise steering. Issigonis was a designer with a real regard for the fundamentals and a liking for simple engineering, so to him a rack-and-pinion system was an almost inevitable choice, as it remained for the Mini, 1100 and other popular Issigonis-designed models.

This 4½-litre boat-tailed Bentley used the typical worm-and-sector steering that was popular for the more powerful cars in the 1920s and 1930s

Steering boxes

In spite of the Citroen/VW/Issigonis examples, most other designers were slow to discard their familiar but less efficient boxes. The worm-and-nut unit actually took on a new lease of life in the late 1940s when the big US specialist manufacturers improved it in the guise of the recirculating-ball principle. By giving the worm-and-nut grooves of part-circular section and putting bearing balls in these grooves—with an external tube to complete the circuit—they replaced sliding contact by rolling contact, with a significant reduction in steering effort; this represented a great improvement also in the unit's wear characteristics.

When produced to normal tolerances, however, recirculating-ball worm-and-nut boxes still had some backlash which made them less precise (especially round the straight-ahead position) than rack-and-pinion systems. Nevertheless, boxes of this type soon came into widespread use, one of the first makers on this side of the Atlantic being the British Burman company whose product was specified for the 1952 Vauxhall E model. The Japanese car manufacturers took up the recirculating-ball box with enthusiasm and not until the end of the 1970s (well behind the Europeans) did they really begin to go over to rack-and-pinion.

A much revered and popular car, Issigonis' Morris Minor also offered its driver the benefits of rack-and-pinion steering

The end of the kingpin

Another steering change brought about by the advent of independent front suspension was the disappearance of the kingpin—the pin that is mounted in each end of a beam front axle and carries the steering swivel. Some designers retained kingpins initially but this meant separate pivots with longitudinal axes to allow the wishbones to articulate, but ball joints (which could cater for both steering and suspension movements) soon took over, thus providing joint specialists such as Automotive Products with a lot of new business.

In the early days, when few cars were fitted with front-wheel brakes, kingpins were usually more or less vertical when seen from ahead. The adoption of front brakes then compelled designers to move the pins farther inboard, so they had to incline them to avoid too big an offset between the tyre contact area and where the kingpin axis met the road. A heavy offset meant too much tendency to deflect the steering if the braking grip was not the same on both sides of the car or if a front tyre should deflate.

For many years, a small positive offset was standard practice and was believed by some to help steering feel. Citroën's revolutionary DS19 of the 1950s broke new ground here, however, by having 'centre-point steering' in which the steering axis of each front wheel met the ground at the centre of the tyre contact patch instead of inboard of it. This layout was claimed to increase steering stability and to reduce tyre scrub during steering manoeuvres.

In 1972, Audi's design and development went further by giving the new front-drive Audi 80 'negative scrub radius' or offset, taking the steering axis outboard of the tyre contact centre. In this way, they gave the steering a self-correcting effect in braking and acceleration on transversely inconsistent surfaces or in the event of tyre failure. A few other makers followed suit but the layout has not gained general approval since it gives the steering an unusual feel and, owing to the considerable inclination of the swivel axes, a tendency to 'flop over' towards full lock.

Power-assisted steering

Back in the 1920s, tank designers began to adopt hydraulic power assistance of the track-steering system to reduce the considerable effort required of the driver. Around ten years later, some of the builders of heavy trucks in the US offered such assistance on certain models but no one seemed very enthusiastic at the time.

However, when the first new-generation US cars were being designed and developed after the Second World War, it was clear that one of the key points was going to be giving the driver the least possible work to do. Even recirculating-ball worm-and-nut boxes were not reducing the steering effort sufficiently, so power-assistance had to be the answer, and one of those who worked hard to make it practicable across the Atlantic was Pierce Arrow's Francis W. Davis. Before long the specialist companies there—notably Ross and Saginaw—designed power-assisted systems, and Cadillac and Chrysler were offering them by 1950. Component makers in Europe—Burman in Britain and ZF in Germany among them—soon followed the American lead, although (since the cars were in general less heavy) their emphasis was on raising the gearing for quicker response rather than reducing the amount of effort required.

Rack-and-pinion steering was originally left out of the power-assistance trend because it was then being applied only to light to medium-weight cars which did not need it. However, Citroën started the fashion for their DS models and other makers—particularly those of heavy, high-performance cars such as Aston Martin—decided that the French company had the right idea. Adwest Engineering, which had taken over the old Marles company, were one of the first to announce an integral power-assisted rack-and-pinion design.

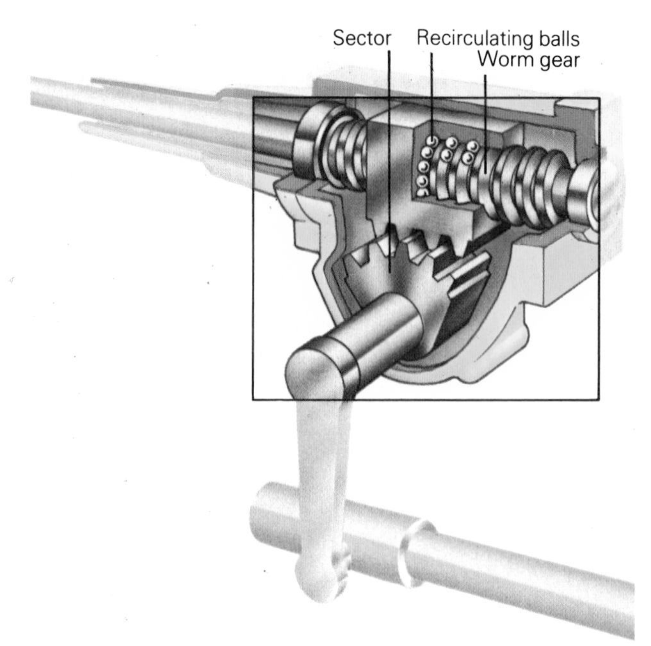

Rack-and-pinion steering was not adopted universally, though. Worm gearing was revived in the recirculating ball design

The case for power steering. Without some servo assistance manoeuvring this 1950s Cadillac would have been virtually impossible

BODY DESIGN

The protective steel cage and front and rear energy-absorbing zones of the Volvo 244 are typical of modern safety requirements

An awareness of public taste and inclination has often proved more vital for the successful designer than the use of new techniques and materials. However, a few men have been gifted and brave enough to take new directions in design.

The car that almost signalled the end of the specialist coachbuilders craft—Henry Ford's 'Tin Lizzie' Model T

In Europe, the two forward-looking car manufacturers had different and most advanced notions about body design. In Paris, André Citroen began building fully enclosed, all-steel bodies for the cars which were rolling out of what had formerly been his munitions factory. This was at a time when the majority of cars were still open-bodied, although the French had early adopted a more practical attitude to motoring and looked for improved weather protection in the form of fixed or detachable roofs. This had given rise to some interesting body forms, including the apparently contradictory Coupe de Ville, with open front seats and enclosed rear ones, and the Landaulette model, with enclosed front seats and open rear ones. Such extravagances were not for Citroen, who saw more profit and a wider market in keeping to the kind of body the self-driving middle-class would want. He did at least offer his *conduite interieure* cars in a variety of colours, unlike Henry Ford whose customers had to be content with black.

Meanwhile, Vicenzo Lancia was entering more advanced thoughts still. He decided to do away with the conventional chassis altogether and build a body after the fashion (it is said) of an ocean liner, with its own inherent rigidity. To this body could be bolted the engine, the driveline and suspension. The resulting car, the Lambda, was neither success nor failure. It was appreciated by enough buyers that it, and its successors, made money and a reputation for Lancia; but other car manufacturers were very slow to follow its lesson. This was despite the fact that the Lambda by virtue of its construction was low-slung and clean-shaped, the thing other manufacturers, especially of sports cars, were trying to achieve.

The early Citroen 2CV was an extremely cheap and very basic design that enabled many people to own a car

While the mass-market was moving slowly in the direction of closed cars, there was still a big demand for open cars, especially sports cars from companies like Bugatti and Alfa Romeo. These retained the separate chassis and were clothed with lightweight bodies.

Citroen and Renault might have been producing cheap enclosed cars in France, but in Britain the new generation was begun by Herbert Austin's little Seven, built down to a price and using a largely traditional structure (with a notably weak chassis). The Seven is noteworthy, however, because it represents a determined attempt, perhaps for the first time, to build a minimum acceptable body round four seats. As initially introduced it was very minimal indeed, but it was also one of the first cars to highlight a second trend in body development, that of the steady increase in size, weight and capability—the 'face-lifting' of an existing design.

The American influences

Meanwhile, across the Atlantic a large motor industry was growing to oppose Ford's dominance, and to take advantage of the increasingly affluent market there. While largely retaining traditional methods of construction, American designers more than most sought to achieve two effects: the apparent lowering of the car, and the beginning of a more rounded appearance—not to be confused with genuine streamlining. While many American designs of the 1920s and 1930s are undistinguished, some superb and even pioneering shapes came from companies at the top end of the market, such as Duesenberg and most of all Cord, the latter with its still-unique appearance and first use of retractable headlamps. Another trend which originated in the US was the design of 'station wagon' (estate car) derivatives of production saloon cars, the first example being the Ford Model A Wagon of 1929.

The European changes

It was, however, in Europe that the next great design breakthrough came, with the arrival of the Citroen Traction Avant. Up until then Citroen, while using advanced production techniques, had kept to rather angular, starchy bodies. With the Traction all that changed, and with the aid of his new designer Emilio Bertoni, Citroen took a leap ahead of all the opposition— even Lancia. The new car took advantage not only of unitary construction—the integration of chassis and body as pioneered by Lancia—but also of front-wheel drive. By eliminating not only the chassis but also the propeller shaft and rear axle, Bertoni managed to design a car which provided as much room as its competitors, yet with less frontal area and a lower centre of gravity. He also arrived at a very good aerodynamic shape, and as a result the Traction was faster, more economical and far better-handling than its rivals. Citroen himself, alas, was too close to illness and death to appreciate the full importance of his car (which was to remain in production until 1955); but Bertoni continued with the company and eventually designed the Traction's equally epoch-making successor, the DS.

The new styles

In America, the trend towards rounded shapes continued until one company—Chrysler—took boldness too far. In 1935 they launched the Airflow,

The Austin Seven was an early attempt to provide a small family saloon that could seat four people in some comfort allied to rugged construction and mechanical reliability

a design which was all curves and which was at least supposedly carried out along genuinely aerodynamic principles. In the market, the Airflow was a disaster and brought Chrysler to the brink of financial ruin. Other American manufacturers contented themselves with adopting unitary construction as soon as it made economic sense, but took care not to offend their customers by changing their shapes too quickly.

Once the Second World War was over, two design trends became clear. In relatively prosperous America, cars were quickly to become large and impressive. In much poorer Europe there was a new interest in small economy cars which encouraged more adventurous thinking and design.

The most obvious change in America was that car bodies were now nearly all-enveloping, lacking running boards altogether and with hardly any distinction between the wings and the main body. As a result of this joining together of the front wings and the body, the traditional upright radiator looked awkwardly small and designers took to wide, low horizontal front grilles.

In Europe two key designs were the Citroen 2CV and the Volkswagen 'Beetle'. They had both been designed just before the Second World War, but neither entered full production until after it was over. The little Citroen had been designed specifically to provide the French peasant class with economical, comfortable and reliable transport; the Volkswagen was conceived by Ferdinand Porsche as a 'universal car' for the German people. Oddly enough, the two cars had other things in common: air-cooled engines, and a self-contained 'platform' chassis which seemed a step back from fully integral construction. Their success, however, was undoubted.

The 1937 Cord 812 was a highly innovative design and was the first car to use retractable headlights

As the tidal wave of war receded, many design experiments took place. Traditional sports car design suffered the shock of Jaguar's XK120, aerodynamically styled by the gifted Malcolm Sayer who died tragically young, and of the Triumph TR series. Mercedes showed that gull-wing doors could be made to work in their 300SL. Lotus, guided by Colin Chapman, proved that clean and beautiful bodies could be made of glass-reinforced plastic (GRP) as well as metal. Ford in America decided a car could be styled by a combination of public opinion research and committee, ended up with the Edsel, and realized they were wrong, for the model was a spectacular failure. At the other extreme General Motors (GM) worked hard to develop a team of gifted stylists, some of whose work (led by William Mitchell) produced in the Buick Riviera and similar cars the most attractive of all post-war American designs. Ford, however, were not without their own success once the Edsel was behind them. They came back with the Mustang, which proved that a new type of car—in this case the 'speciality car', a sort of large and more practical sports car—could be produced using largely existing components, and given its new personality by suitable body design alone.

Today all designers are working hard to produce cars which are above all energy-saving and are, therefore, working outside the scope of pure aesthetics. There is a new interest in weight-saving, in aerodynamics and even in reducing the amount of energy needed to build a car, as well as to run it. Many of these influences are going to change the shape of future cars quite significantly, as low-drag studies from companies like Pinifarina have already shown. Thus it will be even more important that the body designer acts as part of a team together with engineers and energy specialists to produce the car that we will drive tomorrow derived from the many lessons of the earlier days of motoring.

The Fiat Dino, with its exciting bodywork by the legendary Pininfarina, illustrated the advantages of specialist stylists

AERODYNAMICS

When motoring enthusiasts argue about the origins of the modern car's characteristics, they seldom pursue their thoughts beyond the narrow confines of their own interests. However, for even the most blinkered car enthusiast acknowledges that the science of aerodynamics grew from the work of early aviation pioneers. But did it?

Aerodynamics was in fact being studied more than a century before the work of Orville and Wilbur Wright by ballisticians concerned with the accurate trajectories of their artillery projectiles. Those Napoleonic scientists who tried so hard to serve their nation's soldiers suffered a great deal of frustration in their work. They did not have much to go on, bar the theorem that had been propounded by the Swiss mathematician and engineer Daniel Bernoulli, whose principle states that the faster a gas (such as air) moves relative to a solid body, the lower its pressure. Unfortunately, Bernoulli's theorem did not help the ballisticians a great deal, for it failed to explain aerodynamic drag: as far as their classical mathematics allowed them to tell, the pressure of air behind a cannonball in flight was exactly the same as the pressure in front of it so why did it slow down?

The influence of early aircraft design

It was the notion that air could be a viscous medium that was missing from the work of all those early scientists who persistently thought of it as a frictionless fluid. The argument had been by no means resolved by the turn of the century when Dr. Frederick Lanchester wrote his epoch-making study of aerodynamics.

The value of Lanchester's work on aerodynamics would have been sufficient on its own to have stamped his name in the history of car design. His book on the subject was published in 1907, but was based on a paper written in 1894 in which he set out the basic facts about the drag of an aircraft, earlier

To improve roadholding, this 3-litre BMW used wings on the roof and at the back which were a later feature of the BMW CSL

Left: *Pininfarina's Omega, the product of years of design experience and complicated computer analysis may well be the ultimate in efficiently aerodynamic car shapes*

designers had proposed ideas for streamlining an aircraft, ideas that went back well before powered flight.

Lanchester, however, had been studying the behaviour of ships, and realized that air sets up even more frictional resistance than water; and he maintained, in the face of considerable scepticism, that the friction of air passing over the surfaces of a flying machine (or any other airborne body, for that matter) was of crucial importance. He taught that the drag of a perfectly streamlined aircraft should be no more than that caused by the friction of air passing over its surface and that needed to sustain it in the air: any divergence from the ideal streamlined form would increase resistance by causing eddies in the airflow. Here at last was an effective definition of streamlined form: drag due to the form of a body was greater than friction drag with an unstreamlined body, but form drag was less than friction drag in a streamlined one.

The sceptics prevailed for some time, and it was while Lanchester was waiting for the rest of aviation's brains to catch up with his own that he turned to the design of motor cars. However, by 1904 he began to enjoy some support from a German aerodynamicist, Ludwig Prandtl.

In those days, Germany was the place where the study of aerodynamics was being most earnestly pursued. It was the designers of the Zeppelin airships who replaced the ballisticians of the 19th century as the pacemakers sof aerodynamics. They had a particularly good wind tunnel to help them, run by an engineer named Klemperer. With the aid of this, they determined the ideal streamlined shape as a circular-section torpedo with a pointed nose, a tapering tail, and a critical ratio of length to diameter of 6 to 1, any deviation from which caused increased drag either through turbulence or skin friction. This was the shape which was to be the basis of most attemps to streamline cars in the years that followed; but such attempts were scarcely ever carried through with sufficient confidence or resolve.

The 1937 Panhard Dynamic was an unusual design that shows the 1930s purely visual approach to aerodynamics

Jim Hall's Chaparral 2F, driven at Daytona in 1967 by Mike Spence, exemplifies the early 'informed' approach to aerodynamics

Though it may be obvious today, aerodynamics has not always been accepted as being relevant to the design of motor car bodies. There was always somebody who believed in the principle, but hardly ever did anybody know enough about what he was doing to avoid disappointing results or discouraging side-effects. The trouble with all these early experiments in aerodynamics, many of which were devoted to the streamlining of racing cars in one way or another, was that although they were to some extent effective in reducing drag, they also gave rise to other phenomena that could not be fully understood without a thorough scientific investigation that was quite beyond the scope of private firms, and was to some extent irrelevant to the interest of the aviation industry. The same disadvantages applied to streamlined roadgoing cars, such as those offered to the public (notably in the 1920s) by Rumpler and by Benz in Germany, and by Burney in England. The idea sounded specious enough—Rumpler was a respected academic, while Sir Dennistoun Burney, whose prototype was built in 1928 around a 12/75 Alvis engine, was co-designer of the beautiful R100 airship—but the cars did not look convincing because the public, being entirely ignorant of the real issues involved, thought of streamlining only in stylistic terms that were more relevant to human whims than to aerodynamics as displayed by the majority of cars in production at that time.

Something for nothing

The disappointment suffered by Burney and the others in the 1920s might have been enough to deter all future car designers from their ambitions to cheat the wind; but in the 1930s, Germany was once again a place where the desirability of drag reduction fired the imagination of the public, industry and state alike. On the splendid new autobanhen, where the opportunities for sustained high speed were tempting and where petrol was to be treated as a precious commodity because of its strategic importance to the

Above: *With the combination of a very low drag factor and a re-designed engine, the Alpine V6 GT has emerged as one of the most modern supercars*

revitalized nation, the Germans recognized that there was only one way to go very fast in a very low-powered car or to increase the speed of any car without increasing its power—and that was to streamline the bodywork.

Among the most notable designers to show their hands, and one of the first to earn a reputation as a formalist of academic authority, was Freiherr Konig von Fachsenfeld. He designed the fairly simple streamlined racing body for the huge and traditionally angular SSKL Mercedes-Benz two-seater, thus creating a track racer of enormous speed which incidentally catapulted its driver Manfred von Brauchitsch (son of the distinguished soldier) into stardom. This was just the beginning: the bodies of the technically revolutionary Grand Prix cars (with von Brauchitsch usually at the wheel of one of them) launched by Mercedes-Benz into the racing seasons of 1934 to 1937 inclusive were clearly based on the principles expounded by von Fachsenfeld.

It could be argued that von Fachsenfeld did not merit the adulation that has been heaped upon him in some quarters, that he was more a codifier than a pioneer. Certainly there were great exponents of aerodynamics before him—and there were others who in some ways attracted even more attention among his contemporaries, notably Professors Kamm and Everling, who were among those who were conducting systematic programmes of research into aerodynamics. In fact, there had been strenuous efforts made more than a decade earlier to create streamlined bodies, by bravely individual designers such as Bugatti and Voisin—not to mention all the contenders for the land-speed record, and even such primitives as the Porsche design for the Prince Henry Austro-Daimler. This car's so-called 'tulip' body design, with its concave flanks which made it an interesting precursor of the body designs by Michelotti for NSU and other makers in the 1960s, was intended to give the minimum frontal area while providing room for four occupants.

Aerodynamics finds favour

In time, after a long and shameful forty-odd years, when energy began to run out and criticisms began to pour in, the motor industry discovered that aerodynamics would sell after all. In the meantime, aerodynamic cars would race; and so they did, teaching a lot of lessons to the few who were prepared to learn them, lessons that filled every student's exercise book with fins, spoilers, scoops and wings of every imaginable form and function.

The notion of areodynamically induced downforce to increase roadholding could be traced back through the wings of Grand Prix cars, through those pioneering wings mounted on Jim Hall's Chaparral sports cars, through an even earlier wing mounted above a Porsche by Michael May in 1955, back to the big wings that sprouted from the flanks of Fritz Opel's rocket car in the 1920s. Venturi-bodied Grand Prix cars later sought to achieve the same ends by other and possible more potent means, that could likewise be traced back through the ground-sucker model 2J Chaparral through the original side-podded March Formula 1 car designed by the elegantly thinking Robin Herd, back to that same Opel. Probably the only really new statement of formal importance was made in the late 1950s by Frank Costin, a former aerodynamic flight test engineer with De Havilland. Costin's contributions to car design were many, and all the more valuable than the cavalier treatment they received might suggest, but aerodynamically the most important was his embodiment of the principle of reflex camber in which cars are built to make full use of the aerodynamic advantages of a wedge shape.

Recently, however, the need for an aerodynamically efficient car has been gaining public favour. So much so that more manufacturers like Audi (with their streamlined 100) quote the cd figures of their cars in an attempt to prove their car's worth over another.

Below: *This Fiat 1100 special with bodywork by Savio is typical of several designs, produced during the late 1930s that embodied the design concepts originated in Germany by Professor Kamm*

THE CARS

The 70 cars in this second section have been chosen to represent the most sought-after cars of the post-war period. During this time, designers and engineers broke out of the rut that had led to the automotive stagnation of the '30s and gave rise to the great diversity of the different layouts of the cars illustrated here — the variation of the body styling from the grotesque to the elegant and even the number of cylinders.

Cars like the Ferrari Daytona were built almost regardless of expense and they find a place in collections because, for their time, they were the ultimate statement of fast-car design. This type of car is expensive to buy and even more expensive to restore and preserve, yet it receives the greatest tribute that any man-made object can. As with the greatest paintings, there are plenty of fakes on the market.

At the top end of the spectrum, collectors have been buying modern supercars like the Lamborghini Countach and the Porsche 928 since the day they were announced because they have the character of modern works of art. As it happens, these cars justify their appearance on the road and in the way that they perform. Similar machines like the Alfa Romeo Montreal have a similar attraction and are collectable despite their shortcomings. At the end of the day, collectors' cars cannot be defined. Perhaps collectors seek the undefinable.

A.C. COBRA

1962–1969

The A.C. Cobra came about as a result of two decisions, apparently unrelated, which led to the production of one of the fastest production cars ever built.

The first of these was the decision of the Bristol Aeroplane Company to stop production of the six-cylinder engine that powered the A.C. Ace; the second was the ambition of Carroll Shelby, an American driver who was co-victor at Le Mans in 1959, to build a car to his own exacting specifications in terms of power and performance, but using in the main, a production chassis and standard V8 engine and transmission.

Shelby thought that the A.C. chassis was excellent (the Ace was very successful in U.S. 2-litre production sports racing, and had run well at Le Mans from 1957 to 1959), and decided that the extra torque and power could best be gained by fitting a large American V8; the unit he first chose was the Ford Fairlane 221 cu in (4.2-litre) engine, but soon this was changed for the Ford 260 cu in (4.7-litre) derivative. With suitable uprating of the transmission, wheels and brakes, the car was an immediate success, so arrangements were made for the chassis and body to be made at the A.C. works in Thames Ditton, and then shipped to Santa Fe Springs in the USA for the engine and transmission to be fitted and for the final modifications to be made.

Originally, Cobras were fitted with worm-and-peg steering and transverse leaf spring suspension, which made handling at speed somewhat precarious. But their stopping power was always good; from the start disc brakes were fitted all round. In 1963, a much improved rack-and-pinion steering system was introduced in place of the AC worm and sector type. To complement this wishbones and coil springs replaced the leaf springs.

The performance of the car was breathtaking, with a top speed of 242 km/h (150 mph) and acceleration figures from 0 to 97 km/h (0 to 60 mph) in 4.2 seconds and 0 to 161 km/h (0 to 100 mph) in 10.8 seconds. For Le Mans, a Cobra entered in 1963, and fitted with a hard top, exceeded 290 km/h (180 mph) on the straight.

Obviously, this was a car that was virtually made for the race track, and Shelby himself formed a team to exploit the car's potential. In 1964, his cars were placed 1–2–3 in their class in the Sebring round of the World Sports Car Championship, and GT class wins were gained at Daytona, Le Mans and the Nürburgring in the next year. Shelby, however, was not satisfied, and decided that a Ford 427 cu in (7-litre) engine could be fitted to the Cobra; such an engine could only be raced if sufficient road cars were built for homologation purposes.

Accordingly, customers in 1965 could order a Cobra fitted with the 345 bhp engine that was capable of taking the car from 0 to 161 km/h (0 to 100 mph) in just 8.5 seconds, and on to a top speed in excess of 258 km/h (160 mph).

In Thames Ditton, however, all was not well because the company had concentrated all their production facilities on the Cobra since 1963, and the finished product was very remote from the founding firm. A.C. therefore decided to build and market their own version of the Cobra, fitted with a 345 bhp Ford V8 of 7,016 cc capacity in a bodyshell designed by the Italian coachbuilder Pietro Frua. This car, known as the A.C. 428, was far more refined than the existing 427 and the design was further developed throughout 1967. Some 80 428s were built, the last in 1973. The original Cobra itself went out of production in 1969, and by the 1980s was one of the most sought-after sports cars. This led to the introduction of replica Cobras, which were considerably more costly than the originals in the 1960s.

Overleaf and below: *A non-standard Mk III A.C. Cobra with a 700 bhp twin-turbo engine. Cars as powerful as this need a lot of rubber to keep on the road*

COB 1

ALFA ROMEO GIULIETTA SPYDER

1954–1962

The Giulietta was a tremendous milestone in the history of Alfa Romeo. The company had been in financial trouble since 1933, when it was taken over by the Government.

The Giulietta was introduced in 1954 and was a sensational step as it was Alfa's first mass-produced small car and the first 'shopping' car with twin overhead camshafts. The original 1,290 cc (79 cu in) power unit was successively increased to 1,600, 1,800 and eventually 2,000 cc, and this engine powered most of the Alfa Romeo range.

The Giulietta appeared in four-door, two-door coupe (Sprint) and open-topped Spyder versions designed by the coachbuilder Bertone. Further models from Pininfarina and Zagato were also built, the latter versions scoring a number of competition successes. First appearing in 1954, the Giulietta models were superseded by the larger-engined Giulia in 1962.

The engine was the classic Alfa twin-overhead camshaft four-cylinder unit, which featured a light-alloy cylinder head and crankcase. A 74 x 75 mm bore and stroke gave a total displacement of 1,290 cc (78 cu in), producing a power output of 90 bhp at 6,500 rpm from two twin-choke Weber carburettors. Maximum torque was 12 kg m (87 lb ft) at 4,500 rpm.

All models of the Giulietta used a single dry-plate clutch to connect the engine to a four-speed synchromesh manual gearbox, which was mounted in unit with the in-line engine. Drive was through the rear wheels via a two-piece prop-shaft and a hypoid bevel live rear axle mounted on coil springs, radius arms, and an A-bracket. The independent front suspension was by coil springs and wishbones combined with an anti-roll bar.

The body was a monocoque pressed-steel body-chassis unit, with a 239 cm (7 ft 10 in) wheelbase, a front track of 129 cm (4 ft 2 in) and a slightly narrower rear track of 127 cm (4 ft 1 in). The length was 393 cm (12 ft 10 in) and the weight 895 kg (1,973 lb).

The overall influence of the immensely successful Giulietta range on the company has been enormous, and although Alfa Romeo continued to lose money, this was not the fault of these pretty cars, which actually did much towards putting the company on a sounder financial footing.

By the time production ceased, 35,000 Sprint GT and Veloce Giuliettas had been built, including 14,300 Spyders, plus 2,907 of the faster Spyder Veloce model. Because relatively few Spyders were built, and even less exported, a good specimen must have considerable investment potential for the collector, quite apart from the pleasure that can be derived from owning and driving a taut-handling little classic which can still hold its own in terms of performance against many far newer cars.

ALFA ROMEO MONTREAL

1970–1976

Alfa Romeo's only sports car in the supercar idiom of the last two decades. A reminder of the company's past — it won many sports car championships yet turned its production lines entirely to saloons.

The Montreal followed the familiar path from show car to showroom supercar, but it progressed along it very slowly. Its forerunner, a Bertone show car, appeared in 1965, and a developed version carrying the name Montreal was shown at Expo '67 (in Montreal, hence the model name), but the first production cars did not appear before the Turin Motor Show late in 1970; in the first full production year, 1971, around 700 were built.

The first car had been shown with a 1.6-litre Giulia engine, which at least served to make it a runner, but the production model obviously needed more power. This was provided by a version of the T33 sports-racing car V8, in 80 x 64.5 mm, 2,593 cc (158 cu in) form. This derived from an interim racing unit (the full T33/3 engine was a 3-litre unit developing 440 bhp), adapted and detuned but retaining 'racing characteristics' such as dry-sump lubrication and Spica fuel injection. In the Montreal it was rated at 200 bhp at 6,500 rpm, and proved docile and tractable. Maximum speed was around 220 kmh (135 mph). Transmission was through a ZF five-speed gearbox, with a limited-slip differential.

The coupe body lines suggested that this was a mid-engined car, but surprisingly for a car in this class and the period the V8 was mounted ahead of the cockpit. This was adequate for two people, although the two additional seats that were provided were hardly practical (nor was the luggage accommodation as generous as it might have been in a front-engined car). Like the floorpan, the suspension derived from production saloons and was thoroughly conventional, with a wishbone and coil spring independent arrangement at the front and a live axle at the rear. This might seem anachronistic in a late-1960s design in this class, but Alfa Romeo had a deep fund of experience with live axles.

The car arrived too late to have a competition life as a GT car — earlier in the 1960s this would have seemed a natural role for it, especially as the engine could be restored to its race-tuned state with little complication (i.e., a straightforward exchange, provided homologation conditions could be met!). But the Montreal was late into production, and by the time it appeared in numbers cars such as the Ford GT40 and Lamborghini Miura had proved the feasibility of the mid-engined layout for road cars. Manufacture was entrusted to Bertone, and the cars were built to a high standard, but fewer than half of the planned run of 10,000 was completed before production ended in 1976.

ALLARD J2

1949–1954

Sydney Allard was one of the first constructors to combine the power of large-capacity American engines with European-style chassis, building a series of awesome sports-racing cars which reached their zenith with the potent J2 of the early 1950s.

The first Allard specials on these lines had been built in the 1930s, the very first having a Ford V8 and Bugatti-style bodywork (some of it genuine Bugatti bodywork) on a rudimentary chassis. Replicas were built before the Second World War, then in the second half of the 1940s Allard made a deliberate effort to build and market a series of sports cars from his Clapham premises. Sophisticated they were not, but for a while they were highly successful, and now they are revered.

Now recalled as the archetypal Allard, the J2 came in 1949, looking rugged at a standstill, and brutally rugged on the move. The standard engine was the side-valve Mercury V8, bored and stroked to 4,375 cc (267 cu in) to give 110 bhp. However, an Ardun ohv conversion was devised by Zora Arkus Duntov (later to be involved in the development of a competition version of the Chevrolet Corvette) for the basic 3,917 cc (239 cu in) Mercury V8, and this produced 140 bhp at 4,000 rpm. Most J2s were supplied without engines to US customers, for the simple chassis could be adapted to almost any combination of V8 engine and transmission to match. This made the 'standard specification' Mercury almost academic, and Chrysler, Ford, Oldsmobile and other V8s were fitted. The big Cadillac units were most favoured, and most successful.

The chassis was a braced ladder type, there was a coil spring independent suspension in place of Allard's previous split axle and transverse spring arrangement, while at the rear a de Dion axle was used. Stark bodies with cycle wings at the front seemed absolutely right on these cars. Late cars designated J2X had revised front suspension and engine set slightly further forward in the chassis, with a consequently longer nose.

Over 300 bhp was available from the Cadillac V8, and in this light car that gave astounding acceleration. That was a virtue brave race drivers could exploit, but the general lack of sophistication extending to the detail of a rather flexible chassis tended to make cornering exciting, while the drum brakes were not exactly up to the job. Briefly these Allards, especially the Cad-Allards, dominated US sports car racing. Then cars like the XK Jaguars overwhelmed them — they could corner and stop as well as go! The racing highlights came at Le Mans in 1950, when Sydney Allard and Tom Cole finished third in the 24-hour race, in a 5.4-litre (329 cu in) Cadillac-engined J2. Some 200 J2s were built.

ALVIS TD/TE/TF

1959–1967

The distinguished Alvis TD/TE/TF range was renowned for speed allied to luxury and comfort.

Although their Coventry car factory was destroyed by bombing during the Second World War, Alvis maintained aero engine production in 18 shadow factories and therefore had the facilities to allow early resumption of car production in 1946. Pending a new design, George Lanchester's 1938 12/70 was revived with an enlarged engine as the TA 14 but by 1950 Alvis were ready to replace this with a new car related in style but larger, more luxurious, and more powerful.

This was the six-cylinder TA 21, fitted with a 2,993 cc (182 cu in) engine capable of producing 90 bhp. It was not as fast a car as the pre-war Speed Twenty-five (let alone the potent 4.3-litre derivative of it) nor as dashing in style, but it served to confirm the continuity of the Alvis tradition of fine cars of medium-large substance and medium-sporting style. The faster and more sporting TC 21/100 which was offered in 1954 and 1955 (the TB 21 had been a roadster variant of the TA 21) had 100 bhp and a 161 km/h (100 mph) capability, thanks to a tuned engine, a higher axle ratio, and some development by Alec Issigonis, who would end the decade with his celebrated Mini.

Issigonis was designing a successor, a very advanced car with a V8 engine and fully independent suspension, but the company was too timid to depart radically from their established traditions. Instead, a quite beautiful body designed by the Swiss coachbuilder Graber was commissioned for mounting on the TC 21/100 chassis, and this became known quite simply as the 3-litre Alvis. Not many were made until the engine was modified for 1959: endowed as a result with 120 bhp, the car was tagged as the TD 21.

The TD appealed very strongly to a certain and characteristically British taste. It looked a fast car without being in fact very fast; it looked dashing without the slightest hint of vulgarity; it looked rich without being in any way ostentatious. The Graber body had elegant and very simple lines, and the quality of the finish was just what was expected of a coachbuilt car. These things were what mattered to the company's known customers. In fact the engine was notable only for the fact that its timing chain was driven off the rear of the crankshaft. As for the chassis, its semi-elliptic springing of a live rear axle and the rubber mountings of coil spring front wishbones did more for comfort than for roadholding and handling; it was not until 1964 that the demand for an Alvis that would at least be respectably fast in a straight line was met by the TE 21 or Series III car.

For this, twin SU carburettors were fitted to the engine, which produced 130 bhp; reasonable step-off and comfortable high-speed cruising were reconciled in a 5-speed ZF manual gearbox, although a 3-speed Borg-Warner automatic transmission was also available. The top speed of the TE was over 177 km/h (110 mph), but more was to come. While the management were busy with negotiations which led to the company being taken over by Rover in 1965, the engineers were wringing some more performance out of the car, to create the Series IV or TF 21 for 1966. Now, with a 9:1 compression ratio and three SU carburettors, the engine developed 150 bhp which, coupled with a closer ratio gearbox, gave a top speed in excess of 193 km/h (120 mph). A new option was power-assisted steering, but the chassis remained much the same. The car's sole concession to modernity was an electrically driven cooling fan (pioneered some five years earlier by Bristol), but this was scarcely enough to make customers come, to say nothing of making them stay. In the summer of 1967, production ceased and an illustrious automotive name disappeared.

Alvis TE21. Refined English thoroughbred

ASTON MARTIN DB4

1958–1963

The Aston Martin DB4 was hailed as the most significant new model of the year when it was announced at the London Motor Show in 1958.

At its launch, it looked every inch a thoroughbred, and it remains a great favourite with many enthusiasts today, despite certain designed-in faults which were mostly put to right when the model was superseded by the DB5 in 1963.

The close-coupled four-seater body was developed for Aston Martin, the famous British Newport Pagnell company, by Touring of Milan on their 'Superleggera' or 'Ultralight' principle, with aluminium panels on a steel framework. This was mounted on Aston Martin's first platform chassis, the work of Harold Beach, with a new coil spring and wishbone independent front suspension assembly, but with a non-independent coil-spring rear suspension with trailing arms and a Watts linkage.

The engine, first seen at Le Mans in 1957, was Tadek Marek's new 3,670 cc (224 cu in) all-alloy six-cylinder unit with twin chain-driven overhead camshafts and a claimed output of no less than 240 bhp.

Despite the Superleggera label, the DB4 was a heavy car, scaling 1,347 kg (2,969 lb), but contemporary road tests confirm 0 to 100 km/h (0 to 60 mph) acceleration in around 9 seconds, with a maximum speed close to 230 km/h (140 mph). Aston Martin claimed that it was possible to accelerate the DB4 to 160 km/h (100 mph), and then use the all-round Dunlop disc brakes to stop the car again, in 30 seconds.

Above: *In standard form, the DB4 offered high performance, sleek flowing lines and a purposeful appearance*

The DB4 was developed through five fairly distinct versions, Series 1 to Series 5. However, model identification is complicated by numerous production-life changes and a large number of optional extras, not to mention a short-chassis DB4GT with similar bodywork, a lightweight Zagato-bodied DB4GT, a DB4 Convertible, and a DB4 Vantage, with a three-carburettor engine. Official changes included enlarging the sump capacity from 8.5 to 9.6 litres (15 to 17 pints) in 1960, and then to 11.9 litres (21 pints) in 1961; standardizing the optional oil cooler and making the clutch twin-plate instead of single (in 1961); modifying the front grille (in late 1961); and lengthening the car by some 10 cm (4 in) in late 1962 and at the same time reducing the wheel diameter from 16 to 15 in.

Some series 5 cars were fitted with automatic transmission, and a wide variety of final drive ratios were available; in addition, the manual gearbox could be specified with either a close or wide-ratio gear assembly, but in both cases, this rather unpleasant David Brown four-speed gearbox was superseded by a ZF five-speed unit early in the life of the DB5. Other options included an overdrive (from late 1961), and the fitting of a Vantage or Special engine to the standard model.

The DB4 was discontinued in August 1963, and although only 1,100 were built, examples sell relatively cheaply, and therefore seem a tempting proposition to the collector; but any owner who wants to drive fast and hard instead of merely admiring its looks will have to spend a lot of money on fuel and maintenance.

The following DB5 and DB6 Aston Martins were close derivatives of the DB4. The DB5 used the long-wheelbase DB4 bodyshell, with a 3,995 cc (244 cu in) 282 bhp engine, while the DB6 which came in 1965 was a roomier four-seater on a longer wheelbase. It was equipped to a very high standard, and continued in production until 1971.

Below: *DB4GT had a Zagato lightweight body on a standard short chassis and in road tune had a maximum speed of over 240 km/h (150 mph). On the circuits it was seldom a match for the better GT Ferraris*

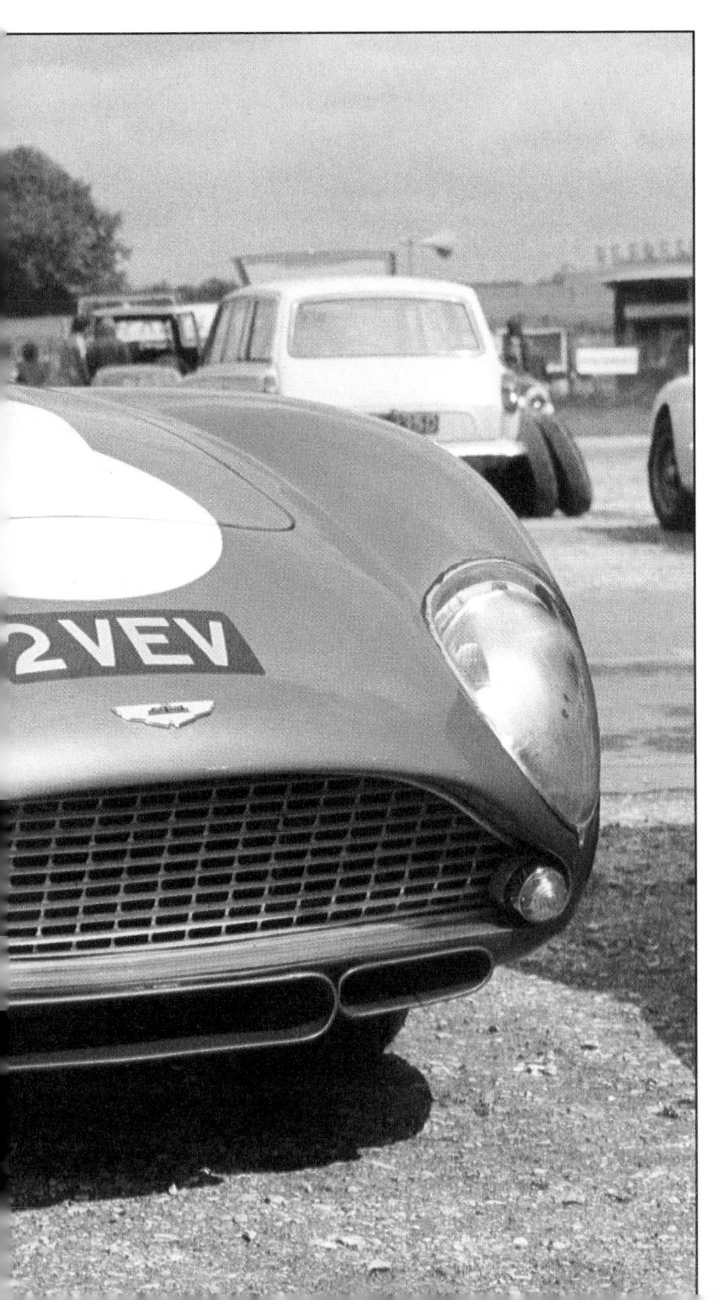

AUSTIN-HEALEY SPRITE

1958–1971

With its distinctive front-end styling that earned it the nickname 'Frog-eye', the Austin-Healey Sprite provided a return to low-cost sports car motoring in the late 1950s.

Introduced in 1958 the Austin-Healey Sprite was designed as a cheap, small sports car using existing BMC stock components. Costing little more than contemporary saloons, it was to complement its larger Austin-Healey stablemate, the 3000, and was welcomed at the time because there was not a quantity-produced sports car in the 1-litre class, and had not been for some time.

The Sprite was powered by the BMC 948 cc (58 cu in) 'A' series engine with twin SU carburettors and double valve springs. There were a number of other modifications made to the valves and bearings to ensure the unit could cope with the claimed 50 bhp output. This gave the car a top speed of 130 kmh (80 mph) and nippy acceleration for its size — it was faster than many of the 1.5 litre family saloons of the time. This was complemented by a good average fuel consumption of 7 litres/100 km (40 mpg). A four-speed gearbox was employed, but the gear ratios were not high enough — it took 13 seconds to reach 80 kmh (50 mph) but an extra 8 seconds to reach 96 kmh (60 mph). It utilised a platform chassis with wishbone front suspension and live rear axle with stiff quarter elliptic springs, and this combined with low weight — 662 kg (1,460 lb) — and low centre of gravity, gave the car good roadholding.

In the spring of 1961 the Mark II Sprite appeared with a completely new body. Gone were the 'frog-eyes' to be replaced with a smart but undistinguished body shape. A year later the car received the 1,098 cc (67 cu in) version of the 'A' series engine to boost the power to 55 bhp and the top speed to 145 kmh (90 mph). It was also available by then with another name, as a badge-engineered M.G. Midget. The Sprite Mark III (Midget Mark II) came in 1964, now with disc brakes and a semi-elliptic rear suspension; 1966 saw the introduction of the Mark IV Sprite (Midget Mark III) with the 1,250 cc (78 cu in) engine.

Austin-Healey production was phased out in 1971 when a total of 129,354 Sprites had been built. The M.G. Midget variant continued, with the Triumph 1,500 cc (91 cu in) engine from 1974, but the original qualities of low cost and good performance had disappeared; production of the Midget ceased in 1979.

Austin-Healey Sprite Mk I. The much loved 'Frog-eye'

AUSTIN-HEALEY 3000

1959–1967

Known as the 'Big Healey', the Austin-Healey 3000 was one of Britain's most successful competition cars in the 1950s and 1960s.

Although the bodywork first appeared in 1956 with the 2.6-litre 100-Six, it is the 3000, launched in the summer of 1959, that is now considered to be the real Big Healey (as opposed to the small Austin-Healey, the Sprite). During its eight year production life, seven distinct types can be traced, all built at Abingdon with bodies manufactured by Jensen.

The Mark I had a revised version of BMC's big straight-six-cylinder engine, with a capacity of 2,912 cc (178 cu in). The 3000 was virtually indistinguishable from the 100-Six; the only external changes were 3000 flashes on the boot lid and on the horizontal-barred front grille. As before, it could be bought as a two-seater (designated the BN7) or as a very cramped occasional four-seater (BT7). The 124 bhp engine of the Mark I provided 0 to 100 km/h (0 to 60 mph) acceleration in just over 11 seconds, and a top speed of 184 km/h (114 mph). Wire wheels, overdrive, and a hard top were available as optional extras, but at first, a brake servo was not.

The Mark II was introduced in June 1961, and was distinguished by a vertical-barred grille; its timing was modified, and three carburettors were fitted to boost the power output to 132 bhp. This model was originally intended for export only, and problems were encountered in tuning the triple carburettors, so eventually there was a return to the tried-and-trusted twin SUs. Another version of the Mark II appeared in September 1962, known as the 3000 Sports Convertible or BJ7, and featured a wrap-around windscreen winding glass windows with quarter vents, and a new hood that was easier to fold and to erect. Mechanical changes included a close-ratio gearbox and a higher final drive. Although in this form the engine gave less power, reduced body drag increased the top speed to 186 km/h (116 mph).

The refining process was taken a step further in February 1964 with the Mark III Convertible (BJ8.I), which had a four-silencer exhaust and a redesigned interior featuring new instruments in a wood-veneered fascia and a full centre console. But there was more to the Mark III than mere cosmetic improvements: larger (2 in) carburettors and a new camshaft raised the power output to 148 bhp, the gearbox ratios were again improved, and a vacuum brake servo was standardized. It now took less than 10 seconds to reach 100 km/h (60 mph) and the maximum speed was increased to 198 km/h (123 mph). A few months later, when only 1,390 of these had been built, two further important changes were made for the BJ8.II: the centre console was lowered to make gear-changing easier, and the chassis frame was cranked downwards at the rear to take different leaf springs and improve the always-poor ground clearance. In this form, it remained in production until late 1967, the last Austin-Healey, despite the fact that a Mark IV prototype had been prepared, fitted with a 4-litre Rolls-Royce engine.

The 'Big Healeys', usually with light-alloy bodies and engines developed to produce up to 210 bhp, were the mainstay of the BMC works rally team through to the mid 1960s, winning 40 class victories in major international events.

The 3000 is a rarer car than some people imagine; of the 42,917 cars built, all but 2,725 were exported. It is not impossibly expensive to buy, but the performance that it gives has to be paid for in terms of noise, discomfort, and substantial fuel consumption. Coupled with its often-unpredictable handling, this makes it a car that is strictly for the enthusiast.

BENTLEY MULSANNE

1982 ONWARD

Walter Owen Bentley himself may have dismissed forced induction as a proper means of increasing engine power but then he never drove a Bentley Mulsanne!

Since 1959, V8-powered Rolls-Royces and their badge-engineered Bentley stablemates have impressed with their luxury and build quality but they have seldom been bought for their performance, that is until the appearance in 1982 of the turbocharged Bentley Mulsanne.

At the heart of the Mulsanne is Roll-Royce's massive and lazy 6,750 cc (412 cu in) all-alloy V8. The exhaust gases from both banks of cylinders are fed at a maximum pressure of 7 psi through a single Garrett AiResearch turbocharger which in turn feeds pressurised combustion mixture to the engine through a single Solex downdraught carburettor. Unlike many other turbo systems, there is no intercooler; the boost pressure is deemed too low for that to be necessary but there is a sophisticated wastegate control which keeps the turbo spinning even when there is no engine loading. This minimises throttle lag when the accelerator is depressed.

Any lag that exists is effectively masked by the smoothness of the General Motors automatic gearbox coupled with the engine's high unboosted natural torque. Rolls-Royce do not divulge power outputs for their engines but admit to a 50 per cent increase for the Mulsanne over its normally aspirated counterpart. An educated guess for the basic unblown power figure is in the region of 200 bhp, so for the Mulsanne, 300 or so seems a fair estimate which can hardly be considered high these days for an engine of such huge displacement, but there is the massive torque to compensate.

The half-shafts are stiffened to cope with the Mulsanne's extra power and the steering is strengthened too. However it may be surprising that the suspension and brakes are left as standard unless customers specify sportier settings.

The most apparent difference between the Mulsanne and the Silver Spirit is the radiator grille which is much lower on the Mulsanne than on the Rolls-Royce version, as well as being painted in body colour as opposed to polished. It should be said that the lower radiator significantly lowers wind resistance and helps the Mulsanne reach a top speed of 220 km/h (135 mph). The limiting factor on top speed is not power or wind resistance, but the resilience of the Avon tyres, which in a car of this bulk take an almost merciless pounding at high velocities. For this reason, the turbo boost is restricted. Were it not, considerably high speeds would doubtless be possible, although quite why anyone would want to travel any faster I can't imagine!

Top speed is one thing; acceleration is another, but the Mulsanne excels in this respect too and its time of 7.3 seconds to 60 mph ranks it as one of the fastest accelerating luxury saloons.

BRISTOL 401

1949–1953

Built by an aeroplane manufacturer, the Bristol 401 was a fresh statement on how a car should be designed.

At the highest levels of musical performance, interpretation can take precedence over composition; something similar applies to cars. Thus when the Cars Division of the Bristol Aeroplane Company had been established after the Second World War as manufacturers of a vehicle that was essentially based on BMW designs, albeit with a great deal of metallurgical and conceptual revisions, they set out in the succeeding model, the 401, to deliver their own fresh statement of how such a car should be devised.

When it appeared in 1949, it was mechanically much the same as the 400, with the same immensely robust A-plan chassis featuring a zero-steering live rear axle sprung by torsion bars, and an independent front suspension combining wishbones and a transverse leaf spring, all jig-tested for accuracy before final assembly so as to complement the exceptionally accurate and high-geared rack-and-pinion steering.

The ride and handling of the 401 reached standards that few other contemporary manufacturers could match. These factors enabled the driver to exploit to the full the 85 bhp and responsiveness of the long-stroke six-cylinder 1,971 cc (120 cu in) engine. This had three downdraught carburettors serving vertical inlet ports between the inclined valves in the hemispherical combustion chambers.

The engine was familiar, but the body was totally new. Designed by Dudley Hobbs, formerly a wing specialist in the Aircraft Division, it was aerodynamically exceptionally efficient, not only in straightforward penetration but also in yaw stability. It was also vastly roomy, had draughtless ventilation, and despite the luxurious finish, it was light in weight. The construction was of aluminium alloy sheet, supported by a network of small diameter tubes.

The top speed was 159 km/h (99 mph) in neutral conditions, but with so slippery a body, the 401 could exceed 161 km/h (100 mph) without much help, and its stamina was tremendous. It enjoyed some successes in rallying and racing, but its true metier was as a full-bodied tourer capable of crossing Europe at very high average speeds.

Like all other cars, it was not beyond criticism. The 4-speed gearbox had very wide ratios, but late models incorporated a closer set featuring Borg-Warner synchromesh in place of the huge Bristol synchronizers, though still with a freewheel incorporated in first gear. The brakes, designed to be used hard, were also designed not to lock up in panic braking, and this made them heavy to operate. The orientation of the roll axis prompted weaving at high speeds when the petrol tank was full. These and other niggles were eradicated when the developed version of the 401, the 100 bhp 403 went into production in 1953, by which time 650 of the 401 had been made. Both are popular with collectors.

CADILLAC FLEETWOOD

1930 ONWARD

Cadillac appeared as a marque as long ago as 1902 and right from the beginning became associated with high-quality, innovative engineering. The Fleetwood model name appeared in 1930 and has persisted ever since.

Antoine de la Mothe Cadillac founded the city of Detroit in 1701, so as a marque name, Cadillac could not really have more historic associations. The name was chosen by Henry Leland for the car that he constructed in 1902 and exhibited at the New York Automobile Show the following year. Despite having only a single-cylinder engine, Leland's products met a ready market and Cadillac entered full-scale production.

By 1930 Cadillac had produced numerous models and established itself firmly as America's leading producer of luxury cars. This was confirmed by the introduction of a remarkable V16-engined model as top of the range and this was accompanied by an outwardly similar car powered by a V12 engine. It was this car that received the Fleetwood name and it seems a shame that this fine V12 seems almost ordinary compared to the V16, an engine configuration that has been seen seldom elsewhere.

The Fleetwood benefitted from Cadillac's innovative policy and it was among the most advanced cars of its time. Cadillac had been one of the first manufacturers to introduce four-wheel brakes, while their 'Synchro-Mesh' gearbox has become common parlance. Similarly the firm was at the forefront of the use of chrome on its cars as well as servo-assisted braking and hydraulic brake operation.

The V12 engine of the Fleetwood gave way to a new V8 unit of 5.7 litres (348 cu in) and 150 bhp in 1936 and it was this engine that the car still had when production was relaunched in 1946 after the interruption of the war. The styling of these first post-war Fleetwoods was carried over from the pre-war cars with an imposing full-width four-door sedan body and unlike, other models in Cadillac's range, the body was not shared with cars made by other General Motors divisions, although it bore familiar similarities. However, it must be stressed that by this time the name Fleetwood was actually being applied to several models within the range although these were all based on a common chassis and had the same engine. Long chassis versions were readily available too.

1948 was a highly significant year in the progression of the Fleetwood, for it was then that the classic American tailfins first appeared as a result, it is said, of Cadillac stylist Harley Earl being rather taken with the tail fins on a Lockhead Lightning P38 aircraft. Initially rather small fins were added, but the trend for bigger and bigger ones grew.

The Fleetwood entered one of its definitive phases in the late 1950s, by which time the styling had been squared off somewhat while lots and lots of chrome had been added.

With fully squared off and elongated styling coming in the 1960s, the Fleetwood in all its body styles reaffirmed its position as the car for presidents and gangland bosses alike with extended multi-seater long-wheelbase versions a common sight. The latest Cadillacs are still impressive vehicles yet they hardly have the same engineering and stylistic integrity of earlier models which is a shame for a marque with such an impeccable pedigree.

1959 Cadillac Fleetwood convertible. Style by the mile

CHEVROLET CORVETTE

1953 ONWARD

The Corvette was a success story for General Motors through the second half of the 1950s, the 1960s and 1970s, and on into the 1980s.

Most Corvettes were distinctive—initially perhaps uninspiring, but then came the second-generation models with characteristic scalloped sides in 1956, the sleeker Sting Ray line from 1963, the masculinity of Mako Shark-inspired body of 1968 which was to last for a decade, the smoother outline of the 1980s. It was by no means always a sports car, but the publicity-inspired tag 'America's Only Sports Car' stuck to it. By American standards it was built in small numbers, the half million mark not being achieved until 24 years after it was introduced.

That introduction came as it was recognized that the post-Second World War American interest in sports cars was not a passing fad. The General Motors heads of styling and engineering, Harvey Earl and Ed Cole, proposed a sports car show model for the 1953 Motorama (a GM travelling exhibition to drum up interest in new models and test reactions to possible projects). The GM management approved, public reaction was positive, and plans to put the Corvette into production were pushed ahead.

Designer Bob McLean had inevitably used many stock parts in his layout, the real novelty for a major manufacturer being a glass-fibre body—the element that made small-quantity production realistic. This was mounted on a very ordinary X-braced box-section chassis, which was to be superseded by a ladder-type frame in 1963. Standard Chevrolet suspension was used, modified at the rear to mount the semi-elliptic springs outside the frame rails (independent rear suspension did not come until the 'Vette had been in existence for 20 years).

The only available engine was a pushrod ohv 3.8-litre (235 cu in) straight-six which was rated at no more than 105 bhp; modifications, including a camshaft from a truck engine, revised head and stronger valve springs, revised induction and three Carter side-draught carburetters, pushed this up to 150 bhp. That was not enough to give real sports car performance—the Corvette came into a market sector where the yardstick was the Jaguar XK120—and it drove through the Powerglide two-speed automatic as there was apparently no suitable manual box in GM's inventory. So there was disappointment that this first Corvette was a roadster or sportster in a long American tradition, but at least its reception confirmed that the market was ready for a sports car.

Zora Arkus-Duntov was responsible for the first transformation. This Belgian-born expatriate Russian was a one-time Allard engineer, and he understood sports cars. Late 1955 Corvettes had a 4.3-litre (265 cu in) V8, then came a three-speed manual gearbox, followed by a 4.6-litre (283 cu in) engine for 1957 and a Borg-Warner four-speed gearbox. Along the way handling was improved, options such as fuel injection (temporarily) and a limited-slip differential became available; in 1958 the familiar quad-headlight nose was introduced.

Meanwhile, Arkus-Duntov had tried to get a proper racing programme off the ground, but this was killed as GM adhered to the Automobile Manufacturers Association ban on racing (officially that remained the line until a GM racing engine was commissioned from a British company in the mid-1980s, although 'assistance' was given to teams like Chaparral). Nevertheless, modified Corvettes per-

Early Corvettes had a bulbous appearance. Fewer than 200 were sold in 1953, when it was nominally available

formed well in the international race at Sebring in 1956 and 1957, and were eighth and tenth at Le Mans in 1960, and were constantly prominent in SCCA national racing in the USA.

A 5,359 cc (327 cu in) V8 giving up to 395 bhp came in 1962, ready for the substantially revised roadster and coupe models with Sting Ray styling in 1963. These were immediately successful, in their appearance and in that Corvette production exceeded 20,000 in a year for the first time, while with the engine in its highest state of tune the first 150 mph (240 km/h) 'Vette appeared. Bigger engines came—up to 7 litres (427 cu in) and 435 bhp for 1966, and then the highly-tuned neo-racing L88 with a claimed 560 bhp—with the essential option of disc brakes on all four wheels or disc front/drum rear.

The next fundamental change came in 1968, again following the lines of a show car styled by William Mitchell (the Mako Shark II of 1965), with the established range of mechanical components, until a new engine, the LT-1, came for 1970. By that time one John Z DeLorean was running Chevrolet's Corvette department. He reduced the number of options offered—by 1973 only three engine options were listed, and they were fairly subdued as 'safety' lobbies and fuel crises swung industry and public sentiment against extreme performance cars—but he did achieve higher production quality. Also the body was refined in detail.

Concept cars still appeared with the name Corvette at motor shows, a mid-engined example arousing expectations about future production 'Vettes, as did two- and four-rotor-engined cars (until GM turned its corporate back on rotary engines). The name—and little more, as 'Corvette GTP'—was however to be applied to a mid-engined sports-racing design which GM commissioned Lola to build for the 1985 IMSA GT race series.

The basic 1968 shape saw out the 1970s: the addition (and subsequent deletion) of spoilers and aerofoils were noticeable outward changes, while there was a hatchback style and 'special edition' versions—usually unflattering paint jobs! By 1981 only one engine was specified, the 5,735 cc (350 cu in) 220 bhp V8, and in a throwback to the first cars there was no catalogued alternative to an automatic.

That model prepared the way for the fourth-generation Corvette. This used the familiar V8, rated at 205 bhp, had plastic transverse leaf springs in its suspension (a novelty introduced on the rear suspension of the preceding model), mild wedge lines in its overall shape, and dimensions and weight measurements close to its European counterparts. 'America's Only Sports Car' was now a GT car.

Above: *Fuel-injected V8-engined 1984 Corvette*

Below: *1958 second-series Corvette with familiar four-headlight nose*

CHEVROLET CAMARO

1966 ONWARD

The Camaro was General Motors' response to the Mustang, conceived in 1964 when GM management had to accept the fact that the Ford was a success and launched in 1966.

Any clash with the Corvette had to be avoided, and because of the time lapse the new GM car had to offer a little more than the Ford in most departments—length, width, interior space, and fittings, and so on. It also had fewer components from the general company parts bin.

In its Z-28 form in 1968–70 the Camaro became one of the leading 'muscle cars' of a brief but fascinating era, and gained a track record to back up its image. Then in 1970 it became a 'pony car', a leader in a pack of new American GT cars. That GT role was filled again by a very different Camaro in the mid-1980s. With the Camaro, Chevrolet adopted a form of construction that was monocoque from the engine firewall back, with the engine itself and front suspension being carried on a sub frame. Suspension was conventional—wishbone and coil spring IFS and live rear axle with semi-elliptics—while most cars had a disc front/drum rear brake combination (all-drum braking was available).

Camaros with the smallest engine offered found new buyers, for a 140 bhp straight six could hardly be regarded as appropriate to this car, and the 155 bhp six-cylinder was little more attractive. The 5,363 cc (327 cu in) V8s rated at 210 bhp and 275 bhp (depending on tune) were a different matter, and at the top there was a 5,740 cc (350 cu in) 295 bhp V8. A 396 cu in (6.5-litre) V8 giving 325 bhp was to follow. The last two were available in the Super Sport Camaro, which also had uprated suspension and a lot of decals and badges to advertise its superiority to other highway users . . .

Real superiority came with the Z-28. This was created for TransAm racing, where the Mustang had ruled. To that end a 4,949 cc (302 cu in) engine was created, to qualify the car within the capacity rules; it produced up to 450 bhp. As a GM company could not be seen to be directly involved in motor sport, the main TransAm effort was handed to the Penske team, which used the Camaro to dominate the 1968–69 seasons.

Revisions for 1970 brought a new smoother body and softer suspension, while the largest V8 offered was the 5,735 cc (350 cu in) unit rated at 300 bhp at 4,800 rpm. This model was raced in the TransAm series by the Chaparral team, with little success in the face of the Boss Mustangs. Camaros reigned on other tracks, however, and their long domination of saloon car racing in Britain was ended only when capacity restrictions ruled them out.

On into the 1970s the Camaro was emasculated as emission controls and other restrictions cut into the power outputs of its engines—ironically, the closely-related 'badge-engineered' Pontiac Firebird came through this period in better shape, its TransAm variant going into the last half of the decade as a survivor of the pony car class. Towards the end of the 1970s the 5.7-litre V8 in the car that still carried the Z-28 designation was rated at a mere 185 bhp at 4,000 rpm.

Early in the 1980s the Z-28 theme became more lively again, and it was still in competition with a Ford Mustang as market sector leader. Top of the range, in prestige and performance terms, came the IROC-Z. This had a 190 bhp 5-litre V8 (for 1985 a 215 bhp version), and as in the 1960s it was sleeker and more handsome than its Ford rival.

CITROEN TRACTION AVANT

1934–1957

'Two years ahead of current motor car construction' was the proud boast with which André Citroen launched his revolutionary front-wheel drive 7CV.

Certainly no other French automobile mass-producer had dared to offer an FWD car at that time, especially at so low a price (it sold in England for £250). Within months it had bankrupted Citroen, whose company was taken over by Michelin in 1934.

The Citroen Traction Avant's elegantly streamlined bodywork was an all-steel integral construction without a separate chassis; the scuttle ended in four 'horns' to which the engine and transmission unit was bolted. Suspension was by torsion bars all round, and was independent at the front. The 1.3-litre (79 cu in) engine, mounted behind the three-speed gearbox (with synchromesh on the upper two ratios), had pushrod-operated overhead valves, a three-bearing crankshaft and detachable cylinder barrels with wet liners.

Inside, despite its low build, the Citroen was outstandingly roomy: the rear seat was 1.22 m (4 ft 2 in) wide, and the fascia-mounted gear lever and umbrella handbrake meant that the front floor was virtually free from obstruction.

Roadholding was outstanding, and the Traction Avant could be cruised at a steady 80 km/h (50 mph); slightly more performance was offered by a 7S version which had increased cylinder bore and 36 bhp compared to the standard 32 bhp. At the end of 1934, both engines had their strokes extended from 80 mm to 100 mm, creating a 1,628 cc (99 cu in), 36 bhp 7CV and 1,911 cc, 46 bhp 11CV, also known as the classic *Onze Legere* and capable of 114–121 km/h (70–75 mph). Early in 1935 came an *Onze Normale* with a choice of two wheelbase lengths allowing for six or eight-seater bodywork.

The Michelin takeover killed off an existing 22CV version of the car with a V8 engine. Distinguished by a redesigned front end with faired-in headlamps, only six were built.

During 1938, a 15CV six-cylinder derivative of the 11CV was launched, its 2.9-litre (177 cu in) engine developing 76 bhp at 3,800 rpm and endowed with a twin-choke downdraught carburettor.

After the war, only saloons were offered. However, the Traction Avant was by this time showing its age, and the 15.6-litres/100 km (18 mpg) petrol consumption of the 15CV was ill-suited to post-war austerity.

During 1954–55, the 15-H model was offered with self-levelling hydro-pneumatic suspension as a curtain-raiser for the revolutionary new DS19 that was to supplant the 15CV Traction Avant at the 1955 Paris Salon after 50,518 examples of the model had been produced. The 11CV survived almost two more years. Total output of the four-cylinder Traction Avants was 708,339.

CITROEN SM

1970–1975

Citroen have never been a company to let technical complexity prevent them from offering a model for sale and the SM was one of the most complicated cars ever made.

Such an advanced up-market model as the SM may have been in the minds of Citroen's product planners for several years before it came to fruition, but it was the takeover of the Italian supercar manufacturer Maserati by Citroen in 1968 that finally paved the way to this exciting car. Citroen saw the advantages of having free access to the specialised technical resources at Maserati and soon after the takeover, the request went out to chief engineer Alfieri at Maserati in Modena for a new V6 engine to power a top-of-the-range Citroen.

Alfieri, a legendary character in Maserati history, rose to the request by suitably modifying a Maserati V8 engine through the simple expedient of removing two of the cylinders. This left a 90° degree V6, which is not the ideal cylinder orientation, but the engine performed well on test, producing, if anything, too much power. Thus it was that the unit was down-sized to give the desired 180 bhp and, with a displacement of 2,670 cc (162 cu in), bring it into a more advantageous car tax bracket in France. Suitably developed, the unit entered production at the Maserati factory for delivery to France.

The mechanical makeup of the SM is typically Citroen, with the engine front mounted, driving the front wheels through a specially developed five-speed gearbox. The suspension is hydropneumatic, driven by an engine-operated pump with the brakes and steering similarly operated by high pressure fluid giving efficient, but incredibly sensitive control. The sensitivity of the controls makes the SM a rather difficult car to drive and some people can never come to terms with the steering which has only two turns lock to lock and variable power which gave a direct 'knife-edge' feeling when travelling in the straight ahead position.

These complicated mechanicals are clothed in a very long and sleek two-door body which has a real supercar appearance. The lines of the car are like an extended version of the CX that followed soon after. While it is undoubtedly a big car, the extent of the interior accommodation is limited and although supposedly a four-seater, the SM should strictly be regarded as a two-plus-two.

The combination of the sleek and aerodynamically efficient body gives the SM a top speed in 217 km/h (135 mph), making it comfortably the fastest ever Citreon while 60 mph is available in 9.3 seconds.

From 1972, SMs were equipped with a larger 3.0-litre engine producing 10 more bhp and these cars were even faster than the first series, being capable of 224 km/h (139 mph) and accelerating to 60 mph in under 9 seconds. Had the car not been geared as a high-speed relaxed cruiser its acceleration would certainly have been much faster.

The handling and ride quality of the SM were universally admired, showing the efficiency of the Citroen-developed suspension system. What defeated the car was its price, for it was always expensive to make; its complexity, which deterred even ardent Citroen devotees; and its thirst for fuel. A two-plus-two car that returned around 14 litres/100 km (20 mpg) in the midst of the first fuel crisis had the odds stacked against it. Rationalisation at Citreon meant that production of the model was transferred to a different factory from the main Citreon works in 1973 and thereafter the numbers built declined.

The final car was built in mid 1975, that being almost the 12,000th example. Soon after, Citroen's interest in Maserati was sold and the company went back to concentrate on more mainstream models. Spinoffs from the project include the use of the SM's engine in the Maserati Merak as well as the car's hydropneumatic suspension, while the gearbox found its way into the mid-engined Lotus Esprit.

DAIMLER MAJESTIC

1958–1969

During the early 1950s, the Daimler Majestic rescued the company's image which had suffered considerably from garish 'specials' inspired by Lady Docker and the subsequent loss of Royal patronage.

When Sir Bernard Docker resigned from the managing directorship in mid-1956 it was time to restore Daimler's tarnished image and one result was the Daimler Majestic of 1958 which was generally rated a much better car than the One-O-Four 3.5-litre (213 cu in) model on which it was based. The new model was re-styled with a lower radiator and full-width bodywork. It could transport six occupants in an atmosphere of polished wood, Connolly leather and thick carpeting. However, the front bench seat was by no means as comfortable as it looked and, by modern standards, the suspension would be considered hard. Surprisingly, automatic chassis lubrication was dropped in favour of separate grease nipples, of which there were 17, all requiring regular routine lubrication.

The six-cylinder engine of the new model also received attention. Its capacity was increased to 3,794 cc (231 cu in) and various other modifications raised the power output to 134.5 bhp at 4,400 rpm. Daimler's traditional fluid-flywheel transmission was replaced by a Borg-Warner 3-speed automatic unit and servo-assisted disc brakes were fitted all round. For a large and heavy car, the Majestic performed well, reaching 90 km/h (60 mph) from rest in about 14 seconds and capable of a genuine 160 km/h (100 mph). With its good brakes, efficient, if low-geared steering and almost roll-free cornering, it covered the road briskly and returned a fuel consumption of around 15.6 litres/100 km (18 mpg), by no means bad for a car of this type.

At the 1959 Motor Show in London, Daimler sprang quite a surprise by showing a prototype of a new model. Known as the Majestic Major, the new car did not enter production until 1961. It looked almost identical to the existing model apart from an extended boot which lengthened the body by 15 cm (6 in). There were changes to the chassis: Dunlop Road Speed tyres were offered as standard, the final drive ratio was raised and Girling power-assisted steering was offered as an option for those who found driving the car too tiring without it.

The main change in the new car lay under the bonnet, where Daimler had installed an enlarged version of the excellent V8 engine used in the SP250 sports model. This big 4,561 cc (278 cu in) unit produced an impressive 220 bhp at 5,500 rpm, and turned the stately Majestic into a 190 km/h (120 mph) car which could reach 90 km/h (60 mph) from rest in only 10 seconds and attain 160 km/h (100 mph) in little over half a minute. Once again, the transmission used by Daimler was a Borg-Warner 3-speed automatic.

The V8 Daimler Majestic saloon would cruise comfortably at the maximum speed of its six-cylinder sister car and had handling and braking to match this performance. Fuel consumption at around 21 litres/100 km (13 mpg) was still not unreasonable and the figure could be increased with moderate driving. A limousine version of the Majestic was available with a wheelbase of 336 cm (132.5 in) and many of these spacious and luxious cars remain in service to this day continuing to provide their owners with exemplary service in the Daimler tradition.

Daimler was taken over by Jaguar in 1960, although Majestic production continued until 1969. Throughout a production life of some 11 years between 1958 and 1969, 3,538 Majestics were made, of which 2,048 were Majestic Majors.

DATSUN 240Z

1969–1973

Rated by many enthusiasts to be the first Japanese car to have potential 'classic' status, the Datsun 240Z was the best-selling sports car in the world in the early 1970s.

Aggressive in its lines, rugged and reliable, with genuine high performance, the 240Z took over a market sector that had been dominated by outwardly similar British models such as the Austin-Healey 3000—indeed, it was sometimes jokingly referred to as 'the last of the big Healeys'.

Nissan had been building sports cars on M.G. lines through the 1960s, but these had been compromise cars and the 240Z was purpose-designed from the outset. Above all, it was tailored for the all-important US market, where 135,000 of the total production of 153,000 were to be sold. Stylist Albrecht Goertz (designer of the BMW 507 sports car in the 1950s) came up with a handsome no-nonsense design which set off a car which proved to have great competition potential. It was only built as a three-door fastback coupe, and the open version which was sometimes rumoured never actually appeared.

One unusual feature for a car of this type was the independent suspension front and rear, by MacPherson strut and lower wishbones. Disc front/drum rear braking was almost automatic. The engine, based on the four-cylinder unit used in Bluebird saloons, was a sohc 2,393 cc (146 cu in) straight six with an ultimate power output of 151 bhp at 5,600 rpm. Four- and five-speed manual gearboxes were offered, and there was an automatic option.

The engine was mounted well forward, and no attempt was made to achieve a 'mid-engined effect', as well-balanced handling was a feature of the car from the outset. The 240Z was also responsive, but the controls were heavy, the ride jarred at low speeds, and the cockpit was noisy. But it had real performance, with a 200 km/h (125 mph) top speed. A more sophisticated 24-valve 2-litre 160 bhp engine was fitted to a few cars in Japan (but apparently none were exported) and this reputedly gave a higher maximum speed.

The 240Z was announced in 1969, and started to make its mark in competition in the following year. In international terms it was best-known as a rally car, and it gratified one of Nissan's prime ambitions by winning the tough East African Safari Rally twice, in 1971 (Hermann and Schuller) and 1973 (Mehta and Doughty). That apart, a third place in the 1972 Monte Carlo Rally was its best placing in a major international, although there were class wins in other events and a victory in the secondary Welsh Rally.

On the circuits the 240Z was never predominant in Europe, but in the USA it won SCCA production sports categories in 1970–71 (Jim Morton) and 1973–74 (Bob Sharp).

Its surprisingly brief production life ended in 1973, when the outwardly very similar 260Z, which promised much but delivered less, took its place. That car was soon superseded by the 280Z, much less sporting in character. Neither had the masculine appeal of the 240Z, and neither made a lasting impression, whereas the exciting 240Z lives on in memory, and is cherished in the metal, as a top-rate sports car.

DE TOMASO PANTERA

1970 ONWARD

A survivor from the first generation of supercars, unusual because it relied on the 'no substitute for cubic inches' approach for the power to give it high performance, and for a while was distributed by a major US company.

Alessandro de Tomaso, Italian-domiciled Argentine and one-time racing driver, had dabbled in high-performance car manufacture for a decade before the Pantera was announced in 1970, building supercars such as the Vallelunga and Mangusta in small numbers. The Mangusta was marketed in the USA and attracted Ford's attention; that in time meant that de Tomaso did not follow conventional Italian supercar lines in his Pantera (Panther), notably in that it used a big Ford V8 rather than a limited-production 'in-house' power unit. Ford's involvement in the project ended in 1974, but the Pantera was still being made a decade later. A price tag around half of that attached to its more extreme contemporaries such as the Lamborghini Countach undoubtedly played a part in that, for the Pantera had almost equal head-turning qualities, and if it fell a little short in outright speed, it was still a very fast car (the maximum ranged from 220 kmh/137 mph to 260 kmh/160 mph, depending on gearing).

The Pantera had a conventional monocoque chassis/body, with a sub frame at the rear to carry engine, transaxle and suspension. As at the front, that was a wishbone and coil spring/damper independent arrangement, and big ventilated disc brakes were fitted front and rear. The associated Ghia styling house was responsible for the sleek lines of the car, which basically remained unchanged through 15 years of production, although later variants sprouted extended wheel arches, nose spoiler and rear wings.

The engine marked the Pantera out. The 5,763 cc (351 cu in) Ford 90-degree pushrod ohv V8 was fitted in two states of tune, producing 330 bhp in the 'L' and 350 bhp in the 'GTS'. Despite emaciating emission controls, that latter figure was maintained in 'high-performance' variants through the 1970s, through such improvements as new manifolds and pistons. Appropriately geared, a Pantera with this V8 returned shattering acceleration figures, albeit this had to be paid for in high consumption (around 24.3 litres/100 km, or 11.6 mpg). By the 1980s, however, the power of the GTS V8 was down to 300 bhp.

The Pantera project had originally been attractive to Ford in the USA as it enabled the company to perpetuate the 'total performance' image that had been cultivated on the backs of the Indianapolis programme and cars like the GT40s in the 1960s. That phase was to pass as cars in that category briefly attracted unwelcome publicity, but meanwhile Ford backed a racing programme for 1971. Bud Moore race-prepared the engines to give more than 400 bhp, which went some way to compensate for the car's weight of more than 1,400 kg (3,080 lb), but the Pantera was never competitive. The works team ran in only two 1000 km races, at Monza and Spa, and in the Le Mans 24-hour Race. This was the important one, of course, but the Panteras hardly brought glory to Ford and the racing programme that had been announced with such heavy publicity somehow just faded away.

It was not really a track machine, rather a well-appointed GT car and largely because of its Ford V8 a practical one, too. By the 1980s production was down to less than a car a week. But it had survived a decade and a half, and by the end of the 20th century the Pantera will have rarity value . . .

FACEL VEGA

1954–1964

The Facel Vega was a car that came about quite literally through the action of another manufacturer for when the French firm Facel Metallon lost a contract to build car bodies, they decided to fill the gap by building their own car instead.

Facel actually stands for *Forges et Ateliers de Construction d'Eure de Loire* and the company went back way beyond the 1950s as suppliers of a wide range of pressed steel components both to the aircraft and automobile industries. The loss of a contract to supply pressed steel bodies for the Dyna-Panhard led to the creation of one of France's few post-war supercars when company boss Jean Daninos laid out plans for a sleek GT car powered by a Chrysler V8 engine.

Under the stylish body was a straightfoward tubular chassis with independent front suspension and a live rear axle. The powerful Chrysler engine, initially of 4.5-litres, was mated to either a Chrysler three-speed automatic gearbox or the strong four-speed Pont-á-Mousson manual gearbox. The car proved itself a hearty performer with a top speed of 210 km/h (130 mph) and while the handling may have been a little basic, this was more than compensated for by the car's poise as a fast motorway cruiser.

This first Facel Vega was known as the FV and just after its introduction came the Facel-Vega 'Excellence' which was broadly similar in concept, but had a four-door pillarless body on a longer wheelbase.

The FV was offered with progressively larger and more powerful Chrysler V8 engines and then in 1959, the car was rebodied to reappear as the HK500 which is probably the definitive Facel Vega and is certainly the most numerous: 490 were finally made.

The HK 500 was altogether larger and heavier than its predecessor and its size led to the specifying of power steering and four-wheel disc brakes. The engine displaced 6.3-litres and with 360 bhp available the car was a formidable performer; top speed was now up to 225 km/h (140 mph). The relatively simple, but enormously effective recipe of using the Chrysler engine was soon followed by other European manufacturers, not least Bristol, Jensen and Gordon-Keeble in Britain and firms such as Iso, De Tomaso, Monteverdi and Monica in Europe.

For the 1962 season in an attempt to bolster flagging sales, the HK 500 was restyled to became the Facel II. The new body was squarer than the old car, while the door pillars became slimmer and the windscreen flattened out somewhat. The mechanicals of the Facel II were in most respects the same as the HK 500 although even more powerful engines could be specified. Coupled with an appropriate rear axle ratio, the Facel could now just top 240 km/h (150 mph), ranking it among the very fastest cars of its day.

The Facel II continued to sell, albeit in small numbers for it was always an expensive car. However, the downfall of Facel Vega had its roots back in 1959 with the introduction of a small 'popular' Facel Vega, known as the Facellia. Despite the lessons learned through the success of fitting a 'bought-out' engine to the big Facels, the firm set about designing their own highly advanced small twin-cam engine for the new car.

The new engine was very effective but was terribly unreliable and it was the crippling cost of developing this unit and lack of sales as a result of its unreliability that brought Facel to their knees in 1964. In the 10 years of its life, fewer than 1,200 of the big V8 Facel Vegas had been made.

Volvo powered Facel Vega. French elegance, Swedish engine

FERRARI 250GT/250GTO

1955–1964

Ferraris are thoroughbreds. Sometimes the adulation for any model with the prancing horse badge is difficult to justify, but the 250GTO was a great car by any standards.

It came into the Ferrari repertoire in the mid-1950s, built around the 60-degree V12 designed by Colombo. Impetus was given to the development of the 250GT line in the aftermath of motor racing's worst accident, at Le Mans in 1955, when one consequence was a move away from out-and-out sports racing cars towards the GT classes. By the time a full international GT championship was established in 1960, 250GTs were numerically dominant in the largest capacity class, and highly successful on the circuits. In 1959, 250GTs with a new body style appeared (one placing third at Le Mans) and later that year this body was mated to a new chassis. The next step was to incorporate the Testa Rossa engine, in its highest state of tune. In 1961 these cars conclusively won the GT championship for Ferrari, and became the basis of the 250GTO.

The regulations called for 100 examples of a GT model to be built in order to achieve homologation (i.e., accepted as eligible to compete in the class as 'production' cars, albeit that production was limited). Ferrari needed the 'O' *(omologato)* to tack onto the 250GT designation, and gained it on the basis that the 250GTO was a variant of the 250GT, despite a production run limited to 40 cars. That caused storms in teacups at the time, although in fact Ferrari was departing little from the letter or spirit of the regulations.

In many respects, the 250GT family was evolutionary. All had a multitubular chassis, with large-section side members, and bodies from leading Italian specialists. The normal alloy body for the 250GT, by Pininfarina, was modified by Ferrari for the 250GTO; the near-flat nose, with its three characteristic half-moon intakes which could be blanked off for fast or cold-weather running, and a rear spoiler helped to gain high-speed stability, one detail where the 250GT had been suspect. The body was admirably set off by Borrani wire wheels. Front suspension was independent, by wishbones (A-arms), coil springs and shock absorbers, but at the rear a live axle was retained, with semi-elliptic springs and supplementary coil springs, and shock absorbers. Disc brakes did not become standard on 250GTs until 1960, but were of course fitted to the 250GTO.

For this car, the sohc V12 was developed to produce around 300 bhp in its 2,953 cc (158 cu in) form. A handful of cars had 390 bhp 3,967 cc (242 cu in) engines. The main-line 3-litre cars had five-speed gearboxes.

So much for the metal. On the circuits the 250GTOs were superb, visually and in the results achieved with them—high overall placings in open sports car races, victories in GT events. In this respect they marked the end of a chapter in Ferrari history, as the company turned away from GT racing. That chapter had been glorious, and private entrants had raced 250GTOs very successfully to uphold the marque's honour and reputation. Needless to say, the 250GTO is a highly prized collectors' car in the 1980s.

Overleaf: *Outstanding even by Ferrari standards, the 250GTO was a very effective racing car. Its derivative marked the point when Ferrari turned whole-heartedly towards the manufacture of refined road cars*

Below: *Beautifully restored Ferrari GT once used by the private racing team, Scuderia Serenissima*

EUP 977B

SUP 500

FIAT DINO

1967–1973

The Fiat Dino was the result of a successful collaboration between Enzo Ferrari and the giant Fiat empire.

The decision to build the Fiat Dino was taken after the announcement of the new regulations for Formula Two racing in 1967; these required that the engines must be derived from a GT car of which no less than 500 were built in the year before its use in racing. Ferrari had developed a V6 engine (partly designed by Dino Ferrari, son of Enzo, who died in 1956; by way of a lasting memorial to his son, Enzo decreed that all Ferrari V6 engines would henceforth bear Dino's name) but the company could in no way reach the 500-unit stipulation. Fiat could mass-produce a high-performance car for the engine and expressed a willingness to do so; the result, a 2-litre Spyder by Pininfarina, was announced at the Turin Motor Show in 1966, but did not actually go into production until May 1967. Soon after, a fastback coupe version by Bertone was added.

Despite the fact the engine was inspired by Ferrari (some changes, notably in the swept capacity, were deemed necessary for mass production), mechanically the Dino was a traditional car. The front engine drove the rear wheels via a 5-speed gearbox, a single dry clutch, and a two-piece propshaft. The front independent suspension featured upper wishbones, coil springs, lower semi-trailing arms, telescopic shock absorbers and an anti-roll bar, while the rear suspension was by means of single leaf springs supporting the live axle, with torque reaction members and—interestingly—two dampers on each side, slightly inclined front and rear.

The capacity of the engine was initially 1,987 cc (121 cu in), and this provided 160 bhp at 7,500 rpm (compared with the 180 bhp of the Ferrari Dino, and the 240 bhp of the racing version with direct fuel injection). However, the Fiat's power was quite adequate for a road car, and gave a top speed of 210 km/h (130 mph) in the Spyder, and 200 km/h (124 mph) in the Coupe version.

In 1968, the Fiat Dino was fitted with electronic transistorized ignition, but in February 1969 production ceased after 3,670 Coupes and 1,163 Spyders had been built.

This was not the end of the Dino story, however, because an improved version of both cars was announced in December of the same year. The major changes were in the capacity of the engine, which was increased to 2,418 cc (147 cu in), and in the new Weber 40DCMF carburettors, which added up to a power increase to 180 bhp at the lower engine speed of 6,600 rpm. The new model exhibited improved torque characteristics, and faster acceleration, although the top speed remained unchanged. A further change was the adoption of strut-type independent rear suspension, modelled on that used on the Fiat 130.

The Dino was extremely well-appointed. An elaborate heating and ventilation system, electric windows, heated rear window, and radio were all standard, and air-conditioning was an optional extra. The popularity of the Fiat Dino was limited only by its high price, because there were few cars in the same mould that could offer such excellent performance in the comfort that the Dino provided, and still achieve an average fuel consumption of 14.7 litres/100 km (19 mpg). In all, 2,398 of the Coupes and 420 of the Spyders were fitted with the 2.4 litre engine.

FORD THUNDERBIRD

1954 ONWARD

Ford launched their T-Bird in 1954 as a 'personal car', and as a counter to the Chevrolet Corvette.

It was never a sports car, although many American enthusiasts hoped that it would be developed into one. That possibility receded later in the 1950s, and although the name remained in Ford catalogues, for two decades it was a label to be applied to unexciting sedans. Then for 1983 the wheel turned almost full circle, for the Thunderbird was re-presented as a 2+2 coupe, with a 2.3-litre (140 cu in) sohc four-cylinder engine which was offered in turbocharged as well as normally-aspirated forms.

The original Thunderbird had been a handsome two-seater roadster, Ford's corporate reaction to the Corvette. In that it was an unquestioned success, outselling the more individualistic Chevrolet by a wide margin. It naturally used stock parts as far as possible, with a braced box-section chassis frame, suspension from a contemporary station wagon, and a 4,785 cc (292 cu in) 198 bhp V8 which normally carried the 'Mercury' label, all clothed in a restrained steel body. Internally it was much more refined than the Corvette, and the penalty that carried in its substantially greater weight was compensated for in the power of its V8.

For 1956 an enlarged V8 (5,112 cc/312 cu in) giving 225 bhp was available, and in 1957 there were four V8 options, up to 5,768 cc (352 cu in) and 300 bhp. In response to the fuel-injected Corvette that year, Ford produced a small number of T-Birds with supercharged 5,112 cc engines, which developed more than 325 bhp.

That was a fleeting high point. Little more than a year later the name was applied to four-seater touring cars—which the buffs disparagingly dubbed 'Squarebird'—and that policy remained through to the 1980s. That decade saw the introduction of the 2+2 coupe, seen as a rival to the larger BMWs, Datsun and Toyota quasi-sports models, or the contemporary Pontiac Firebird as well as the 'old adversary', the Corvette. Its make-up was conventional, with a unitary body/chassis, disc/drum brake combination, MacPherson-type front suspension and live rear axle, and a five speed manual gearbox. In turbocharged form, with Bosch L-Jetronic fuel injection, the engine produced 142 bhp at 5,000 rpm, which gave the 1983 Thunderbird a maximum speed nudging 190 km/h (120 mph). In concept it was very close to the original T-Bird of the mid 1950s . . .

Meanwhile, those early cars had gained in value to collectors, particularly as rust-free examples were scarce. The most prized were the second series cars, of 1956, which had the spare wheel mounted under a shaped cover at the rear of the trunk (this was not altogether a design whim, as luggage space was limited). In 1957 that distinctive spare wheel had given way to a modest tail fin styling. That turned out to be the first step on a downward path for the Thunderbird . . . until the revival in 1983.

1957 Ford Thunderbird. The famous 'T-Bird'

FORD ZEPHYR MK II

1956–1962

The Ford Zephyr and its associated models, the Consul and Zodiac, formed the mainstay of Ford's production right through the 1950s and continued well into the 1960s.

The Mk I Consul and Zephyr were Ford's first new post-war models and were introduced at the 1950 Motor Show in London where understandably they caused quite a stir. Their styling may look quaint and old-fashioned to us now but at the time it was right up to the minute, while the car's internal fittings were well above average for vehicles of the period. The two models were joined by the even better equipped Zodiac in 1953. The Zodiac was fitted with the same six-cylinder engine as the Zephyr, while the Consul had a rather less powerful four-cylinder unit.

By 1956, Ford deemed the time right to introduce a much-revised version of the model and the rounded, dumpy lines of the Mk I Consul, Zephyr, Zodiac was replaced by the longer, sleeker but still curvaceous shape of the Mk II which in various forms was to remain in production until 1962.

The Zephyr version of the range was differentiated from the Consul by its larger full-width grille with a hump in the middle. Also there were bumper over-riders and a different light layout. Zodiacs were similar to the Zephyrs, but had more chrome and a higher level of trim. At 2.6m (104.5 in), the Consul's wheelbase is 6.3 cm (2.5 in) shorter than the Zephyr and Zodiac. As alternatives to the basic saloon body, buyers could specify a stylish convertible version made by Carbodies, or a useful estate design produced by Abbotts. The convertibles are particularly sought after these days.

The engine that powered the Zephyr and Zodiac was simple and strong with a four-bearing crankshaft. Its actual displacement was 2,553 cc (155 cu in) and with a single carburettor produced 90 bhp at 4,400 rpm which was sufficient to give a respectable top speed of 135 km/h (84 mph), with 0–60 mph in 17.9 seconds. The basic gearbox was a three-speed unit with a column gear-change, but from 1957 an automatic gearbox became available. From the same year an overdrive on top gear became optional.

Until 1961, drum brakes were the norm, but from 1961, front disc brakes became optional and then a year later standard equipment, thus boosting the car's stopping power dramatically. These later cars also had a different roof panel pressing, known as the 'low-line'. This was a reflection of a growing demand from the buying public for a lower, more angular shape and with this in mind the new Mk III Zephyrs and Zodiacs of 1962 were completely different bodily with many sharp angles and distinct tail fins. It should be noted however, that the drive train in these later cars was exactly same as that used in the early ones.

Mk II Zephyrs may have had a fairly humble mechanical makeup, but they responded well to tuning and they were above all tough and could stand punishment. On the race circuits of Britain and rally routes throughout the world they achieved considerable success.

FORD LOTUS CORTINA

1963–1966

The Ford Cortina, from its announcement in late 1963, was developed from a 1,200 cc family car into the fire-eating Lotus Cortina.

Colin Chapman, Keith Duckworth of Cosworth engineering and Harry Mundy of Coventry Climax all played a part in designing the twin-cam engine, which had first appeared the previous year in the Lotus 23 that Jim Clark drove indecently fast around the Nürburgring (to the great surprise of rival teams).

Clark, Graham Hill, Sir John Whitmore, Vic Elford, Bengt Soderstorm, Jacky Ickx and even Jackie Stewart were among the big names associated with the Lotus Cortina's many race and rally successes in the years that followed. In all, 3,301 were built before production of the Mk 1 came to an end in late 1966.

Normally, the big-bore 1,558 cc (95 cu in) engine was supplied with a 9.5-to-1 compression ratio and two 40 DCOE Weber carburettors, which produced a 105 bhp at 5,500 rpm and a maximum speed of around 177 km/h (110 mph), but some engines were further developed by BRM to give 145 bhp at 6,500 rpm for saloon racing, and these were capable of exceeding 200 km/h (125 mph) on a high axle ratio.

The suspension was lowered and stiffened, with bracing tubes to the top mountings of the rear coil springs, and the rear axle was located by radius arms and an A-bracket. A really outstanding close-ratio four-speed gearbox was fitted, together with a highly effective vacuum brake servo, although the standard 'umbrella handle' handbrake was retained. The instrumentation was more comprehensive than on standard saloons, a wood-rimmed steering wheel was fitted, and the front seats were re-shaped to give more support when the car was being driven fast.

In the fashion of the legendary Model T, customers were given no choice of paintwork or interior trim; the one-and-only colour scheme for the body was white with a green flash running along the sides and across the tail, and the interior trim was black. To compensate for the added weight elsewhere, the Lotus Cortina had an aluminium bonnet, bootlid and doors (these were easily damaged in use) but the car still weighed some 13.6 kg (30 lb) more than the standard version. Despite the weight penalty, however, the car could still accelerate from 0 to 100 km/h (0 to 60 mph) in around 10 seconds, and the overall fuel consumption was a little above 14.1 litres/100 km (20 mpg), which was not unreasonable considering the car's potential performance.

The Lotus Cortina was twice British Saloon Racing Champion and as such was not best-suited to go shopping in. It was noisy and harsh to drive, with an engine that felt rough below 2,000 rpm and might well oil up its spark plugs in city traffic. This, together with the fact that the car was fitted with a high first gear, meant that some skill with the clutch and throttle pedals was necessary on initial getaway.

The strengthened and stiffened suspension transmitted considerable road noise without entirely eradicating the basic weaknesses of the standard Cortina's roadholding, and this meant that the Lotus Cortina was not such a safe car as the Mini-Cooper in the hands of an inexperienced driver.

FORD GT40

1964–1969

The GT40 was one of Ford's great competitions cars, although ironically when it won it was not as part of the 'works' team.

The Ford Motor Company was committed to 'total performance' in the 1960s, and had to take the plunge into international motor sport to live up to the image its publicists were creating. So Fords ran in the Monte Carlo Rally, their Falcons coming surprisingly close to winning in 1963, and Ford-powered Lotus cars ran at Indianapolis, winning the 500 at the third attempt. In Ford minds there was one other 'classic' international road race to be contested, the Le Mans 24-hour Race. Once committed to a sports-racing programme with that in view, Ford had to win; the irony is that the Ford works teams failed with their first car, the GT40, and succeeded with its successors. In Ford minds, the GT40 was at best obsolescent when it twice won the Le Mans classic . . .

Ford inexperience in this field was recognized so the GT40 operation was based in England, and Eric Broadley of Lola, and others such as experienced team manager John Wyer, were brought into the programme. Broadley had introduced a Lola sports-racing coupe with a mid-mounted Ford V8 early in 1963, on lines close to those which a Ford design team under Roy Lunn had started to explore. So although the Lola GT was by no means a prototype of the Ford GT40, experience with it was to contribute to the Ford design and development phases, underlining the Anglo-American nature of the programme.

The first GT40 was completed in the Spring of 1964, leaving little time for test and development work before its race debut. It was a well-proportioned and sleek mid-engined coupe. The basis of the car was a sheet-metal semi-monocoque centre section, with large box side sills contributing to the strength of the structure and housing the fuel tanks. Steel sub frames for and aft carried the front and rear suspension, and provided mountings for the engine. The glass-fibre bodywork had clean lines, with doors cut into the roof and neat air intakes. However,

spoilers had to be added when handling problems were encountered in the first high-speed tests—one of the shortcomings that had not shown up in wind-tunnel tests. A 4,195 cc (289 cu in) 350 bhp pushrod ohv V8 was fitted, rather than the pure twin-ohc racing V8 originally proposed. Initially, transmission was through a Colotti four-speed gearbox, in unit with the rear axle and final drive, but this proved unreliable and ZF gearboxes were used on later cars.

A batch of 12 prototype GT40s was laid down at the Ford Advanced Vehicles plant at Slough, west of London, for Ford's intention was to honour the letter and spirit of the international race regulations and sell replicas of the car their team raced. Initially the race programme brought disappointment, at least to these Ford executives who had expected victory first time out at Le Mans. At the French circuit the cars had proved their speed in 1964, one setting a new lap record and being timed at 317.8 km/h (197.5 mph) down the long main straight. All three cars retired.

The GT40 was modified for 1965, and an open version was tried. However, Ford attention was increasingly focussed on the Mk II, a derivative powered by a 7-litre version of the Galaxie V8, then after another failure at Le Mans totally towards this car and the all-new Mk IV, to the exclusion of the GT40. Ford Advanced Vehicles under John Wyer had been left to continue GT40 production, and at the end of 1966 Wyer and John Willment were encouraged to take over this operation, continuing GT40 production and servicing as JW Automotive Engineering (JWA). Just over 100 cars were to be built at Slough, although some of these were completed in the USA as Mk IIs, while seven were built as Mk IIIs (a road car equipped to higher standards) and three as Mirages (a 5-litre derivative for the JWA team to race, which became ineligible for international championship racing in 1968, when one was reconverted to a GT40).

In 1967 John Wyer started a racing programme with backing from Gulf Oil, and the GT40 was developed as he felt it should have been two years earlier—he had always been convinced that the car had the potential to win at Le Mans and that the elaborate Mk II and Mk IV operations were not necessary. The team enjoyed considerable success with the GT40 and their Mirage, but in 1968 had to fall back on to the GT40s, using 4.7-litre engines and later a version stroked to 4,992 cc (302 cu in), which gave up to 412 bhp in 1968 and 425 bhp in 1969.

The 1968 season was enormously successful, the JWA team and its season-long rival, Porsche, each going to the final race at Le Mans with four victories behind them. One of the JWA cars became the first GT40 to complete the 24-hour race, and it won. That victory clinched the sports car championship in the name of Ford, who had actually withdrawn from this category of racing after winning at Le Mans with a Mk IV in 1967!

The 3-litre Mirage that was intended to take over from the GT40 in the JWA team progressed very slowly, and the team had to bring out its trusty GT40s again in 1969. Once again the high point was the race at Le Mans, where the GT40s appeared to be totally outclassed by new cars such as the Porsche 917. However, reliability and race experience saw one of the Fords through to victory, by the narrowest of margins. Driven by Jacky Ickx and Jack Oliver, it finished less than 100 metres ahead of a Porsche, having averaged 208.25 km/h (129.41 mph) for the 24 hours. Moreover, two other GT40s finished third and sixth.

That was a remarkable climax to the front-line career of a remarkable car. A decade later its 'classic' status was fully appreciated, values rose enormously and replica GT40s appeared in Britain and Switzerland—Safir Engineering even used the original patterns, jigs and moulds in their version. Some of the original cars which had apparently been written off were painstakingly rebuilt, so that only seven of those that had been built at Slough in the 1960s totally disappeared.

As for Ford, the British company less than wholeheartedly put some effort into 3-litre sports-racing cars, there was the European Ford C-100 project of the 1980s which was axed before it was fully developed, then from Ford in the USA came the impetus for a new mid-engined sports-racing project in the mid-1980s . . .

The GT40 was most successful in the Gulf colours of the JWA team, shown off **(left)** *by Jacky Ickx in the winning car in the 1968 Spa 1000 km race. The Mk III derivative* **(following pages)** *was a half-hearted road car effort—only seven of these cars were built although some GT40s were converted privately for road use*

NDF 2M

FORD MUSTANG

1964 ONWARD

Mustang is another one of those model names its owner seemingly cannot part with: it came into the Ford inventory in 1964 and was still there in 1984, showing every sign of lasting out another decade.

Purists tended to decry the early Mustangs as 'special-bodied Falcons', but that judgement was to be shown to be very hollow, and ironically that first chunky body is perhaps the best-recalled Mustang style, unpretentious but effective.

The Mustang came in 1964 to fill the gap for a sporting car in Ford's range—very successfully, too, in that a million were sold in two years. Its mechanical elements—engines, transmission and running gear—came from the Falcon, Fairlane, Galaxie and Mercury Comet. A platform chassis was used, with body panels welded to it, while suspension was a conventional IFS/live rear axle combination. Initially three engine options were offered, a 2.8-litre (172 cu in) 101 bhp straight six and V8s of 4.2 litres (257 cu in) and 4.7 litres (288 cu in) giving 164 bhp and 210 bhp respectively. Quite deliberately, there was no attempt to repeat the two-seater configuration of the early Thunderbird 'personal car'—the Mustang was a four-seater, in hard-top coupe, convertible and fastback coupe forms.

Inevitably in the 1960s, higher performance was sought for a car in this quasi-sporting category, way over and above the 'Rally Pac' (clock and rev counter!) or 'Special Handling Package' (uprated-springs, shock absorber and front roll bar), or the optional (!) disc brakes offered by the factory. In competitions, the Mustang was a four-seater and thus regarded as a saloon, and as such it was to be very successful on European circuits, while Alan Mann team cars won the 1964 Tour de France.

Shelby American really made a circuit car of the Mustang, taking the fastback body of 1964 as the basis, removing the two rear seats to take it out of the saloon categories and tuning it to a high degree: revised suspension and steering, wide wheels, limited-slip differential and amongst other things a lot more power. In its best-known form, as the Shelby GT-350, it had a 289 cu in (5.7 litre) V8,

Top: *Shelby GT-350 gave the Mustang a performance image never attained with the standard cars*
Above: *Introduced in 1973, the Mach 1 Mustang became one of the less successful Mustang models*
Below: *In its first form the Mustang was immensely successful, although it hardly lived up to its 'sporting' image*

giving just over 300 bhp in street form, nearing 400 bhp when competition prepared (nominally 350 bhp, hence the designation).

Late GT-350s were built by Ford and the 'go-faster' elements were largely cosmetic, but the Bud Moore-tuned Boss Mustangs run in TransAm races around 1970 maintained the Mustang image. In 1973 the Mustang Mach 1 was introduced in three body types. This Mustang was not particularly popular because of its poor power to weight ratio.

The Mustang image slipped further with the Pinto-based Mustang II of the mid-1970s, which had 2.3-litre (141 cu in) and 2.6-litre (159 cu in) V6 engines, or a 5-litre V8. A new small Mustang which came in 1978 used these engines, but on the smallest the option of a Garrett AiResearch turbocharger was offered, boosting output to a respectable 118 bhp.

By the early 1980s the Mustang was being described as a musclecar, for the years when 'power' and 'performance' were dirty words were beginning to recede. In 1984 the 5-litre V8 used in the Mustang was producing 210 bhp, drove through a close-ratio five-speed gearbox, while the car had appropriate uprated suspension and looked the part, fitting easily into the internationally recognized GT category. Nevertheless, the abiding impression of Ford's Mustang is of the Shelby or Moore quasi-works cars in action on race circuits more than a decade earlier.

GILBERN INVADER

1970–1974

The Gilbern Invader was a very stylish car made for the individualist by a very individual company.

Founded in 1959, the Welsh company of Gilbern numbered many ex-miners in its workforce and while production never rose above a handful of cars per week, the factory earned a reputation for high standards of design, manufacture and assembly. In common with many small manufacturers of the period, a large proportion of the cars were sold as kits thus allowing the buyer to avoid the purchase tax attracted by vehicles sold fully assembled.

Conceived as a genuine 2+2 fast tourer, the Invader fulfilled the requirement very well. It was long-legged, fun to drive and distinctive. Replacing the Genie in 1970, the Invader's glass-fibre body was built, in true Gilbern tradition, on a tubular steel chassis that was extended where necessary to provide firm mountings for door hinges, safety belts and the boot lock.

Both the chassis and the body were built by Gilbern themselves while the engine and gearbox were bought in from Ford. The Invader used the Zodiac's 3-litre (183 cu in) V6 unit and four-speed gearbox and only minor modifications (a re-designed exhaust and a wire gauze air cleaner) were sufficient to boost the power output to 144 bhp. Laycock overdrive was available on both third and top gears to give the car crisper acceleration and a greater top speed—0 to 90 km/h (0 to 60 mph) in 9 seconds with top speed of 185 km/h (115 mph)—while a small number of Invaders were fitted with Borg-Warner automatic transmission. The earliest Invaders used independent front suspension from the MGC and a live rear axle with trailing arms and Panhard rod. The brakes were from Girling—discs at the front with drums at the rear. Within a matter of months of the Mark 1 came the Mark 2, the most important change in design being the introduction of Gilbern's own independent front suspension.

The Invader was very much a driving enthusiast's car. Contemporary testers criticized its heavy low-speed steering and harsh ride but praised its open road nature. At high speed, the car was direct and responsive with the positive feel of the rack and pinion steering encouraging the driver to make full use of the car's ample power. This, combined with the fact that the car adequately fulfilled its touring function by affording great comfort to four adults on a long trip, created a most favourable overall impression.

An estate version of the Invader was introduced in 1971, while the Mark 3 was announced the following year. Though similar in appearance to its predecessors, the Mark 3 was nevertheless 50 mm (2 in) wider, and used wide section tyres on 330 mm (13 in) rims as opposed to the 380 mm (15 in) rims fitted to the Marks 1 and 2. Performance was improved significantly, the top speed being raised to 210 km/h (130 mph) and the 0 to 90 km/h (0 to 60 mph) figure cut to 7.2 seconds.

However, the company was running into financial difficulties. The overdrive-equipped Mark 1 had gone on sale at £2,490 fully assembled and the Mark 3 at £2,693. Competitors, particularly the Ford Capri and MGBGT, considerably undercut these figures and Gilbern sales declined. The introduction of VAT forced Gilbern to abandon kit cars with the announcement of the Mark 3 and safety regulations, coupled with rising fuel prices, finally forced the factory to close in 1974. Factory records unfortunately have been lost but production totals are estimated at Marks 1 and 2, 394 units (including 68 estates); Mark 3, 191 units.

GORDON-KEEBLE

1964–1966

When, after a long gestation period, the Gordon-Keeble eventually came on the market in 1964 it was known as the IT, the initials standing for International Touring at a time when the makers felt that the letters GT for Grand Touring had been too greatly abused by the mass producers.

In fact the car was the grandest of tourers, a genuine four-seater with good luggage accommodation and a stupendous performance. Up to 115 km/h (70 mph) it could keep up with the quickest of E-type Jaguars, up to 160 km/h (100 mph) with the DB5 Aston Martin (a matter of 19.6 seconds), and its maximum speed was in excess of 225 km/h (140 mph).

The brakes were of matching excellence, achieving up to 1.1 g retardation with the help of high-speed cross-ply tyres by Avon, which also contributed to good roadholding and exceptionally good traction. Most of the credit for this however was due to the rear suspension, of De Dion type with the dead axle beam located by two pairs of parallel trailing links and a transverse Watt linkage. Had the coil spring and wishbone front suspension been equally good, the car's roadholding, handling and steering might have been superb instead of merely good. As it was, really spirited cornering made the front wheels assume some rather improvident angles, and the low-geared steering called for a lot of arm movement and hard work. The chassis was a space frame of electrically-welded square tubes.

The driver also had a rather burdensome task in manipulating the awkwardly-placed gear lever for the GM 4-speed synchromesh gearbox. This could be hard work when the car was new, but a high-mileage specimen could offer a delightfully light and swift gear change that could be accomplished without the use of the clutch. The gearbox had to be robust because it was transmitting the torque of a 5,355 cc (326 cu in) Chevrolet V8 engine in what GM called 'intermediate' tune, which signified 300 bhp.

It was not only brute force that made the Gordon-Keeble a very fast car; it was light, and the bodywork, styled by Bertone, was reasonably compact and quite sleek. Bertone's prototype had been in steel, but the production cars were bodied in GRP, produced by Williams and Pritchard to a higher standard of quality than had ever been seen before. The passenger configuration was elaborately insulated against sound, heat and vibration.

The total production run was scarcely more than a few; when the firm finally closed down financial problems that were no fault either of the car or the management—save that the GK1 was consistently underpriced—only 99 had been built. Management changes were numerous—John Gordon (at whose behest Jim Keeble had designed the space frame) gave way to George Wansborough; Harold Smith followed until mid-1967 and last owner De Bruyne saw the company through to its demise in 1968, when it carried his name during its last months and a second model (the Grand Sport) was announced. The irony lay in the use of a tortoise as a radiator badge: the Gordon-Keeble was reasonably fast, but then again tortoises live longer.

JAGUAR XK120

1948–1954

The London Motor Show of 1948 was a significant event in many respects—above all, it saw the introduction of a new-engine, Jaguar's now legendary XK six-cylinder twin overhead camshaft unit, and a new sports car, the XK120.

From their sidecar manufacturing origins of 1922, William Lyons' company progressed to the first SS cars, a series of Standard-based cars which were rather more rakish in appearance than performance. With their name changed to Jaguar Cars Ltd, they went to the Earls Court Show equipped with the new engine and a new model.

The six-cylinder XK engine had a bore of 83 mm and a stroke of 106 mm, giving a swept volume of 3,442 cc (210 cu in). A pair of overhead camshafts, inclined at 70 degrees, were driven by a two-stage roller chain and the high-tensile aluminium alloy cylinder head was attached to a chrome-iron cylinder block. Two 1.75 in SU carburettors were fitted and a minimum power output of 150 bhp at 5,500 rpm was claimed.

To utilize the six-cylinder engine, William Lyons initially envisaged a limited production run of 200 aluminium-bodied sports cars. When the XK120 was unveiled at Earls Court, however, it soon

NUB 120 was one of the most famous of XK120s, being rallied with great success throughout Europe by Ian Appleyard

Left-hand drive XK120 taking part in an historic sports car race at Brands Hatch

became apparent that a limited production run would be incapable of satisfying demand for the two-seater and enthusiasts flocked to the Jaguar stand to gaze at the car's striking lines.

The basis of the XK 120 was a hefty box-section chassis of high rigidity. The front suspension was independent, by means of torsion bars and wide-based wishbones while a live rear axle was employed, supported by semi-elliptic leaf springs. Recirculating ball steering was used and braking was achieved by 30.5 cm (12 in), hydraulically-operated drums. These were to prove one of the few weak points of the car, and disc brakes were later introduced.

After the original production batch of 200 cars, models were equipped with steel bodies in the interests of price and ease of manufacture.

With its outstanding performance characteristics, the XK120 soon appeared on racing circuits. In August 1949 the new model took first and second places at the Silverstone One Hour Production car race. Further victories were recorded in the Tourist Trophy, the Tulip and RAC Rallies and the Liege-Rome-Liege Rally, all in 1951.

In 1951 the two-seater was joined by a handsome fixed-head coupé and the following year a more powerful 'Special Equipment' model was introduced. A drophead coupé was announced in 1953 but in 1954 XK120 production ceased when the XK140 was introduced.

For performance, the XK120 had few rivals, certainly at the price; in 1949 a standard production model was timed at 204 km/h (126.5 mph) on the Jabbeke autoroute in Belgium despite having the hood and sidescreens in place. In 1953 a stripped and modified version, with a perspex bubble over the cockpit, was timed at 277.5 km/h (172.41 mph), the fastest speed the model ever recorded. But perhaps its most impressive performance came at the Montlhéry track in France where a standard fixed-head coupé averaged over 161 km/h (100 mph) for a week.

A true production sports car, the XK120 inspired a motoring generation and sired Jaguar's first purpose-built racing model, the C type, which was instrumental in establishing the company's racing reputation.

JAGUAR MK II

1959–1969

The 1959 London Motor Show marked the turning point when Jaguar's first unitary construction model, the Mark I, finally came of age in the form of the Mark II.

The slightly tapered look of the Mark I was alleviated by endowing the Mark II with a wider rear track and the glass area was increased dramatically, and with beneficial effect, by a return to doors with very slim chromium metal pillars and the incorporation of a larger rear screen.

The Mark II range used the familiar 2,483 cc (151 cu in) and 3,442 cc (210 cu in) XK six-cylinder twin overhead camshaft engines producing 120 bhp and 210 bhp respectively, and these were supplemented by a 3,781 cc (231 cu in) 220 bhp version. The compression ratio was 8 to 1, although alternative ratios of 7 or 9 to 1 could be specified.

Disc brakes were standard on all four wheels; disc wheels were also standard wear but attractive wire wheels were a popular option. Front suspension was by double wishbones and coil springs, while the live rear axle was located very securely by quarter-elliptic, inverted leaf springs, two torque arms and a Panhard rod. Burman recirculating ball steering was employed and power-assistance became an option, greatly reducing the amount of wheel twirling demanded from the driver. A Thornton Powr-Lok limited-slip differential was standard on the 3.8 and optional on the 3.4.

One of the debits of pre-1965 models was the Moss gearbox which had synchromesh on the upper three ratios but not on first. A definite one-pause-two technique was essential if silent changes were to be effected and the gear lever movements were extremely long and ponderous. Overdrive was a worthwhile option and most manual models were so equipped. With it, fuel consumption on a 2.4 was in the region of 16.5 to 11.7 litres/km (17 to 24 mpg), while an overdrive 3.8 could achieve 18.8 to 12.8 litres/km (15 to 22 mpg). Automatic transmission could also be specified.

Performance was really the metier of the 3.4 and 3.8 models; a manual 3.8 could accelerate from a standstill to 97 km/h (60 mph) in 8.5 seconds, reached 161 km/h (100 mph) in 25.1 seconds and was capable of a genuine 202 km/h (125 mph).

The lines of the Mark II were complemented by lavish interior appointments: leather seats, comprehensive instrumentation and walnut fascias being common to all models.

In 1965 a new all-synchromesh gearbox was introduced, giving much improved selection and a quicker gear change. In 1967 the Mark IIs were modified slightly to incorporate slim-line bumpers and, in the cheaper models, Ambla upholstery. Such standard items as fog lamps were deleted from the cars' specification but this was accompanied by a price reduction for some models.

The 240/340 models, as they were known, were stop-gap models, and remained in production until 1968 (340) and 1969 (240), their successors being the XJ range. During its lifetime the Mark II sired the superficially similar S type and 420 models, the latter marketed also as Daimlers, while a 2½-litre Daimler V8 engine was installed in a Mark II bodyshell and sold for some years as the Daimler 2½-litre/250. Altogether, some 90,000 Mark IIs were manufactured between 1959 and 1969.

The outstanding performance of the 3.8 made it a firm favourite with racing and rally drivers and for four seasons the model held sway as the dominant machine in production saloon car racing. A 3.8 broke four International Class C records on the banked circuit at Monza in Northern Italy, including 10,000 km (6,210 miles) of continuous high-speed running at an average speed of 171.5 km/h (106.58 mph).

JAGUAR E-TYPE

1961 – 1975

Jaguar launched the E-type in March 1961 in open two-seater or fixed-head coupe form. It proved an immediate sensation.

Its XK engine, originally developed for the Mk VII sports saloon, and later used in both the C and D-types, was a six-cylinder twin overhead cam in-line unit which featured hemispherical combustion chambers. The 3,781 cc (231 cu in) unit was fed by triple SU carburettors and delivered no less than 220 bhp at 5,500 rpm, and this power output permitted a top speed of just under 240 km/h (150 mph). This was matched by acceleration from 0 to 161 km/h (0 to 100 mph) in just 19 seconds, a figure which few contemporary cars could beat.

The chassis closely followed D-type practice. It was constructed in two sections, the first being a tubular steel frame which supported the engine and front suspension; this frame was bolted to a stout bulkhead, which formed the front of the second section, a monocoque which extended to the rear of the car and housed the driver, the final drive, and the rear suspension. It was the rear suspension that represented the biggest single departure from the D-type layout, as for the E-type a new and outstanding all-independent assembly was designed.

E-type production fell into three distinct phases: the 3.8-litre model from 1961–1964: 4.2-litre cars from 1964–1971: and the 5.3-litre V12-engined examples from 1971–1975.

The gearbox of the 3.8 had come in for some criticism, as it was rather slow and difficult to operate smoothly. For the first of the 4.2-litre models therefore, this component was drastically re-designed. Tagged the 'Series 1', the 4.2 was bored out to 4,235 cc (258 cu in), and this caused a few problems, as the positions of the cylinders had to be juggled slightly.

The year 1966 saw the introduction of a third body style, the 2+2; a longer wheelbase and re-designed cockpit allowed more room for rear seat passengers, but to some eyes, the higher roofline destroyed the flowing lines of the car. Looming US emission control and safety regulations forced a number of revisions, first in 1967. Most notable of these minor changes was the removal of the Triplex screens over the headlamps (such cars are often referred to as 'Series 1½'). October 1968 brought, with the start of Series 2 production, an E-type fully equipped to meet the US Federal restrictions, although the outward appearance of the car was little changed.

The Series 3 E-type marked marked the debut of Jaguar's V12 engine, a 60-degree unit (5,343 cc/326 cu in) which produced 272 bhp at 5,850 rpm. Its size caused minor revision of the front sub-frame and suspension, but the most striking change lay in the completely revised bodywork. This model was available in just two forms: the roadster (with optional hardtop) and the 2+2.

Jaguar never officially entered six-cylinder E-types in competition, but actively assisted private entrants. The cars lost out in early tussles with the very fast 250 GT Ferraris, but gained fourth and fifth places at Le Mans in 1962. In the following year, Jaguar began production of 12 'lightweight' E-types but despite having the services of drivers such as Graham Hill and Jackie Stewart, these cars never achieved substantial successes. The factory's refusal to become fully involved in their development was a major cause of the failure; Jaguar's US division proved that the cars could be competitive by backing a pair of very successful 5.3-litre cars, run by the Group 44 team, which took the 1975 SCCA title. Sadly, this classic British sports car went out of production in late 1975, after 72,507 had been built.

Series 3 E-type **(left)** *had a longer wheelbase than the Series 1 cars* **(following pages),** *to accommodate the V12 engine and 2+2 body*

JDU 877E

JAGUAR XJ-S

1975 ONWARD

Introduced in 1975, the XJ-S was the natural successor to the immortal E-Type but the new car was every inch the luxury GT rather than a sports car.

Admiration of the new XJ-S was by no means universal in 1975, the critics fondly remembering how beautiful and dramatic the E-Type had seemed when it first appeared 14 years before. Indeed there was something flawed about the XJ-S's styling, especially around the rear window but once people sampled the car's dynamic qualities, such misgivings were soon forgotten.

The XJ-S was fitted with a version of the powerful 12-cylinder 'vee' engine that had also been fitted to final models of the E-Type. This engine was a productionised version of the unit that engineers Harry Mundy and Walter Hassan had designed for the stillborn Jaguar XJ-13 Le Mans racing car project. This car was actually built and proved itself to be very fast, but it never raced.

The racing engine had quadruple camshafts, but for the road-going engine, two of these were dispensed with, leaving a single camshaft per bank of cylinders. The block and cylinder head were of light alloy and in XJ-S guise the engine had Bosch-Lucas fuel injection which enabled it to produce a smooth and relaxed 285 bhp.

In 1981 a revised version of the V12 was introduced, known as the 'HE' or High Efficiency design. This produced even more power and torque but, through careful design of the combustion chambers, consumed significantly less fuel than the standard engine. Then in 1983, the XJ-S became available with an all-new 3.6-litre (219 cu in) six-cylinder engine and at the same time a 'cabriolet' option was added to the XJ-S range although specialist coachbuilding firms had been converting cars from the beginning.

By far the majority of XJ-Ss were built with automatic transmission, the popular General Motors type-400 three-speed unit. However, up until 1979 buyers could specify the fitting of Jaguar's own four-speed manual gearbox. Surprisingly, relatively few manual cars were built which is a shame because the silky smooth and delightfully powerful engine is at its best when the driver can choose the gears and revs. On the other hand, the unit's tremendous torque ensures that the XJ-S is still a sparkling performer, even with the auto 'box.

Top speed is in the region of 240 km/h (150 mph) and acceleration to 100 km/h (60 mph) takes a little over 7 seconds which is truly impressive for a car of this size and level of comfort. However, this does not tell the full story because it is not what the Jaguar does that makes it such an impressive car, but the way in which it does it. It has great poise and there is little harshness, even under fierce acceleration.

The car's handling under normal conditions is exemplary too and it is only in really hard driving on twisty roads that any shortcomings in the suspension manifest themselves by way of body 'float' and a feeling that you are making the car go faster than it really wants to.

The XJ-S is, of course, still in production but is widely regarded as a 'current classic' and early versions are already collectable. In the very best Jaguar traditions it offers an unbeatable amalgam of those three virtues expounded in Jaguar advertisements for so many years; Grace, Pace and Space!

JENSEN CV8

1962–1967

The Jensen CV8 was designed as a competitor to the E-type and is now a highly sought after collectors car.

In the 1960s a number of manufacturers were in competition to produce increasingly more powerful, faster, luxury cars, with fuel consumption regarded as an irrelevance. In the UK the most popular was the Jaguar E-type, but other manufacturers such as Bristol, Aston Martin, AC Cars, and Jensen found a ready market for cars which were very expensive to buy, extremely expensive to run and in many respects, rather impractical.

Of all the cars made by Jensen, the most coveted by collectors is the CV8 which during its five-year life broke new ground on several fronts. From the start it had glass-fibre bodywork on a chassis made of two longitudinal steel tubes linked by sheet metal cross-members. This method was chosen to allow relatively simple modification of the chassis for future models.

For the previous model, the 541, Jensen had used Austin engines and gearboxes, but such was the race for power and speed that an American Chrysler 5.9-litre (360 cu in) V8 unit was chosen for the Mark 1 version of the CV8. This unit produced 305 bhp at 4,600 rpm on a 9:1 compression ratio, and allied with a Chrysler Torqueflite automatic gearbox, gave the car a top speed of around 210 km/h (130 mph) and a 0 to 80 km/h (0 to 50 mph) time of about 6 seconds. Later versions of the Jensen CV8 were fitted with a slightly more powerful 6.2-litre (378 cu in) version of the same American Chrysler engine.

The total number of CV8s produced was only 496 according to the company records, and this low level of production allowed considerable flexibility. Jensen produced Marks I, II, and III, as well as a number of CV8s with manual transmission and, more interestingly,a few with four-wheel drive using the Ferguson system. The latter were effectively prototypes for the short-lived Jensen FF, part of the Interceptor range which followed the CV8 as the Jensen company headed towards financial crises and ultimate collapse.

With hindsight, the CV8 was one of the highest peaks attained by the Jensen company. By comparison with its predecessor, it was 45 kg (100 lb) lighter, considerably faster, and technically much more advanced. It was one of the first production cars fitted with disc brakes on all four wheels, it had a limited-slip differential as standard, and other features such as reclining seats, two-speed wipers with washers, reversing lights and a radio which were rare original equipment fittings in 1962.

It paved the way for the first high performance four-wheel drive car to be put into production, and it was only financial weakness and the start of a dramatic change in motoring fashion that killed the company: at best a CV8 did no better than 21.6 litres/100 km (13 mpg).

All Jensens are sought by enthusiasts, and a service and spares network continues to operate from the former factory, while in 1984 limited production was resumed by Jensen Cars Ltd, at the rate of one Interceptor a month.

JOWETT JAVELIN

1947–1953

The Javelin was an aerodynamically and mechanically advanced model that the Jowett Car Company hoped would sell well after the Second World War.

As early as 1942, the company recruited a new chief designer, Gerald Palmer, to work on the car. Because the factory was situated in Bradford, it had escaped the devastation of the motor manufacturing centres of Birmingham and Coventry as a result of the wartime bombing, and Palmer was therefore able to proceed unhindered with the development of a compact yet roomy six-seater with good ground clearance, aimed at the motorist who was looking for something a little more luxurious and mechanically more sophisticated than Jowett's mass-producing competitors could offer.

Following Jowett tradition, a horizontally-opposed engine was used; not only did the company have the expertise to build a new engine, they were also confident that it would sell, as their earlier 7 hp flat-twin engine, first used in 1905, was at the time still in production, and remained so until the company ceased trading in 1953. But though the new power unit followed a long tradition, it was anything but old-fashioned in design, for it was the first British power unit to be die-cast from light alloy, with wet liners of cast-iron. Hydraulic tappets and overhead valves were a complete departure from previous Jowett practice. This 1,486 cc (91 cu in) engine was initially rated at 50 bhp, but by 1950 had been uprated to 60 bhp at 4,750 rpm. In the Jupiter sports car, introduced in 1950 using Javelin mechanical components, it was rated at 62.5 bhp or 70 bhp in competition tune.

The suspension featured torsion bars all round, with independent springing at the front which, combined with a unitary chassis construction, endowed the car with excellent roadholding and ride. Launched in 1947, the Javelin soon proved its worth in competition; a works-entered Javelin won the 1.5-litre class in the 1949 Monte Carlo Rally, driven by Palmer, T. C. Wise and T. C. Harrison. In the same year, a Javelin won the 1.5-litre class in the Spa 24 Hours race.

The Javelin found favour too with ordinary motorists and the motoring press, who reported a top speed of around 129 km/h (80 mph) coupled with fuel consumption of 9.4 litres/100 km (30 mpg), and praised the quality of the ride and the handling. Sales improved from just 31 Javelins in 1947 to a peak of 5,769 in 1951 but thereafter Jowett made the fatal mistake of trying to build their own gearboxes instead of buying them as before. The new gearboxes often failed, giving the Javelin a reputation for unreliability, and orders fell, leaving the company with a vast stockpile of cars.

Jowett's body builder was taken over by a major manufacturer in 1953, and although production was maintained at a trickle to the end of that year the failure to find an alternative source of bodies, coupled with ever-increasing warranty claims and loss of confidence, finally overwhelmed the company; production of the Javelin had to be suspended in 1953 and the company was sold to International Harvester in 1954.

LAGONDA RAPIDE

1961–1964

The Lagonda Rapide was aimed at perfectionists and was dubbed 'the finest of the fast cars'.

When the Lagonda 3-litre ceased production in 1958, the marque disappeared from world markets. In 1961, however, the reason for its absence became clear with the introduction of the new Rapide. Three years of continuous development had satisfied the exacting Sir David Brown that his new luxury express, designed to 'invade the future audaciously', was ready for production.

The Rapide—reviving a name popularized on some 1930s 4½-litre Lagondas—was powered by an enlarged version of the Aston Martin DB4's twin-overhead camshaft, six-cylinder engine. The bore and stroke of 96 by 92 mm resulted in a capacity of 3,995 cc (244 cu in), the unit producing 236 bhp at 5,000 rpm and 265 lb ft of torque at 4,000 rpm. Two twin-choke Solex sidedraught carburettors were employed, fed by twin fuel pumps mounted under the rear seat. Twin fuel tanks were also a feature, with a single filler flap operated electromagnetically from a control by the driver's seat. In a successful effort to reduce decibels, no less than six exhaust silencers were used. An automatic gearbox was standard, but a four-speed manual unit was an option.

The striking bodywork was designed by Carrozzeria Touring of Milan and built on their 'Superleggera' principle. The chassis was a steel platform, with a superstructure of light alloy panels attached directly to a network of small-diameter 'birdcage' tubes welded to it.

At the front the car featured coil spring suspension with servo-assisted Dunlop disc brakes. At the rear, however, the company drew on their racing experience gained with the Aston Martin DB3S and DBR1-300 models, using a de Dion axle with transverse torsion bars, lever arm dampers and a Watts linkage. The brakes were again discs, but the centre-lock disc wheels were an unusual feature.

The sophisticated rear suspension and 50/50 weight distribution endowed the rapide with impressive road manners, enhanced by rack-and-pinion steering. Performance was most impressive too, with a 0 to 100 mph (161 km/h) time of 26.1 seconds (for a car weighing 3,780 lb/1720 kg) and a top speed of over 201 km/h (125 mph). Fuel consumption was in the region of 18.8 to 15.6 litres/100 km (15 to 18 mpg).

The Rapide was a large car, with an overall length of 496.6 cm (16 ft 3.5 in), width of 176.5 cm (5ft 9.5 in) and a 289.6 cm (9 ft 6in) wheelbase. The compactness of the de Dion rear suspension and the location of the fuel tanks in the rear wings ensured that rear seat passengers had more than adequate leg room, and the hide upholstery enhanced their comfort. The front seats had a reclining facility, and the standard electrically operated windows, radio and electric aerial added to the air of opulence. Picnic tables were provided in the rear, and the central armrest housed a powder compact, a cigarette case and even a comb.

Although cheaper than contemporary Rolls-Royce models, the Rapide was not a success. Production continued until 1964 but by then demand for Aston Martins required the Rapide's space in the Newport Pagnell factory and the handsome model was deleted after a mere 60 had been made. Once again 'Lagonda' lapsed, until it was revived for an Aston Martin model in the 1980s.

LAMBORGHINI MIURA

1966–1972

New standards were set when Lamborghini introduced a mid-engined supercar in 1966, the P400 Miura, the first of the type to be put into serious production.

Ferruccio Lamborghini entered the motor industry in the early 1960s with front-engined cars, the 3.5-litre 350GT and 4-litre 400GT, that were not outstandingly handsome or successful. But the V12 that was fitted to them was both. Based on a Bizzarini racing design, it was a conventional 60-degree twin overhead camshaft unit that seemed to the automotive world to have been built to be developed for racing. It was not, nor were the cars it powered, and it was a source of disappointment to enthusiasts in the 1960s that Lamborghini did not extend his challenge to Ferrari to the circuits.

In 1965 the 4-litre engine (82 x 62 mm, 3,929 cc/240 cu in) appeared in a show chassis, mounted transversely ahead of the rear wheels. The tendency was to admire designer Gianpaolo Dallara's ingenuity and dismiss the car as a show extravaganza. But during the winter of 1965–66 that chassis was clothed in a sensational two-seater coupe body by Bertone, and with only minor modification and refinement it was to be put into production as the P400 Miura ('fighting bull', echoing Lamborghini's zodiac sign). The Miura was to be built until 1972, some 1,200 being completed before it was succeeded by the equally sensational Countach.

It had a straightforward punt-type chassis to carry the elegant light-alloy bodywork, and there was independent suspension to all four wheels by wishbones, coil springs, dampers and anti-roll bars. Power transmission to the five-speed gearbox was of necessity via a gear-driven connection. The nose section and engine cover were hinged at front and back, lifting to give first-class access, and somewhat limited luggage space was provided in the nose and right at the back.

The V12 was initially rated at 350 bhp at 7,700 rpm, which gave the Miura a top speed of over 270 kmh (170 mph), and during the life of the car it was twice uprated, to give 370 bhp in the P400S of 1969 and 385 bhp at 7,850 rpm in the P400SV of 1971. The potential to enlarge it to 5 litres was designed in, but never needed in the Miura for this car could match its rivals for acceleration and speed, as well as in ride, roadholding and braking. Nevertheless, it could not be regarded as a docile car, and called for respect if most (let alone all) of its performance potential was to be exploited.

To the astonishment of virtually everybody who saw the original Lamborghini mid-engined exhibit at the 1965 Turin Motor Show, the Miura turned out to be a practical GT supercar. Like any landmark car, its status and value will not diminish as its origins fade from memory . . .

Previous page and left:
Trend-setting Miura was thoroughly practical, for example in the access to its engine—shown on the preceding page—as well as elegant and very fast

LAMBORGHINI COUNTACH

1971 ONWARD

The ultimate supercar of the 1970s, a dream car that turned out to be a practical road car with shattering performance, in production for more than decade.

When the first Countach was exhibited on the Bertone stand at the Geneva Motor Show in 1971 few regarded it as anything more than a sleek and futuristic but impractical show car intended to demonstrate the coachbuilder's artistry. Yet this advanced styling exercise was developed into a production reality, and it continued to be built by Lamborghini through years of company crises in the late 1970s and on into the 1980s — it was still marketed in 1985, as a 273 kmh (170 mph) supercar. Production had been intermittent and volume was low (around 500 cars in the first ten years), but this extraordinary machine was available, at a price; it was encountered on highways, and carefully maintained examples were obviously destined to become collectors' pieces before the end of the 20th century.

Lamborghini did not start production until two years after the first Countach was shown, and although the first-series cars looked similar to the prototype there were many changes under the skin. A tubular space frame was used in place of the original monocoque, with wishbone and coil spring independent suspension all round.

The first engine was a 60-degree twin-ohc V12 of 3,929 cc (240 cu in) with six twin-choke Weber carburettors which looked mightily impressive when the rear deck was raised, and more to the point was rated at 375 bhp at 8,000 rpm (almost 100 bhp/litre). In an effort to maintain a near-even weight distribution, the five-speed gearbox was positioned ahead of the V12, with a shaft running back to the final drive. The large fuel tanks were also positioned centrally in the interests of weight distribution, one in each flank alongside the cockpit (each had a capacity of 40 litres/13.2 Imp gal).

This first Countach maintained Lamborghini's reputation for cars with excellent handling qualities to back up performance — the estimated maximum speed was 175 mph, short of the claimed 190 mph but not by much, and wildly in excess of open-road speed limits in much of the world! The overall lines of the original show car were retained, although flush air intakes appeared on the sides. Access was through doors which were hinged at the front and opened upwards. The cockpit was practical, and road visibility forwards was surprisingly good, although there were large blind areas to the rear.

The LP400 gave way to the Countach S in 1978, with some body modifications and the option of flamboyant extended wheel arches and a rear 'wing' as well as braking and suspension refinements. In 1982 the Countach LP500S was introduced, with the bore and stroke of the V12 increased to give a capacity of 4,754 cc (290 cu in). The claimed maximum power was still 375 bhp, but at 7,000 rpm instead of 8,000 rpm, while the torque characteristics were considerably improved. The estimated top speed was still around 170 mph, with acceleration to match (for example, 0–160 kmh/0–100 mph in 11.3 seconds). In any language, at any stage of its history, the Countach was a super car . . .

Right and overleaf: *The Countach seemed improbable when it was first shown, but this futuristic supercar actually reached production, and proved to be a grand tourer without peer in some respects*

LANCIA FULVIA COUPÉ

1965–1976

In 1965, Lancia introduced the Fulvia Coupe, a derivative of the Fulvia sedan that was to remain in production for 11 years.

Produced in several variants, it became best-known and recognized in its 1.3S and 1.6HF forms.

The Coupe version of the Fulvia was strikingly different from its box-like predecessor. Breaking from the Lancia tradition of having outside stylists design the sporting versions of basic models, the Coupe was designed in-house with the intial brief that it was not to exceed 4,000 mm (13 ft 8 in) in length or 900 kg (1,984 lb) in weight, while providing comfortable seating for two with at least restricted space for two more.

As far as final products ever conform to their original specification, the Coupe did so. At 3,975 mm (156 in) it just undercut its length specification though it weighed 70 kg (156 lb) more than was intended. The SA1 Coupe, made from 1965 to early 1970, was produced with three slightly different engines, each mated to a four-speed gearbox. The first cars to roll off the production line were equipped with a 80 bhp 1,216 cc (74 cu in) unit, this later being enlarged to 1,298 cc (79 cu in) to give first 87 bhp, and then 93 bhp. In its ultimate form, the V4 engine was taken out to 1,584 cc (97 cu in) to give a very respectable 114 bhp at 6,000 rpm.

The most obvious of changes in other areas was the new five-speed gearbox with its Ferrari-like gate. First gear was away to the left and down, second was a dog-leg to the right and the remainder combined to form the conventional H with reverse directly above first. This layout gave the driver the opportunity, once the car was actually rolling, to move through the remaining four close ratios with the inconvenience of only one dog-leg change instead of the more usual two on a five-speed car. Another change on the S2 was the move away from Dunlop disc brakes to four-pot Girling units.

For the Series 3 cars, made from early 1974 to the demise of the Fulvia in 1976, only minor cosmetic changes to the design were made. The powerful, narrow V-4 twin-carburetted engine and the gearbox remained unchanged.

In competition the Fulvia Coupe has had notable successes, most scored by a 1.6 litre competition version (Sandro Munari's win on the 1972 Monte Carlo rally for example). The more streamlined Zagato-styled variant was less successful on the circuits.

In total, 138,300 S1, 2 and 3 Fulvia Coupes were produced. With their aesthetic appeal (enhanced by the raised outer headlamps of later UK models) and commendable fuel consumption of 10.8 litres/100 km (26 mpg) in town and around 7.4 litres/100 km (38 mpg) on high-speed runs these 2+2 models from Turin have become cars to collect for the enthusiast and investors alike.

LINCOLN CONTINENTAL

1940–1948

The origins of Lincoln go back to the early 1920s, when Henry M. Leland left the Cadillac company he had created, and introduced another grand car under the name Lincoln.

The company lasted little more than a year after the car was introduced, and it was rescued by Ford. That company maintained the Lincoln line of large 'quality' cars through the 1920s, challenging Cadillac and others for top-of-the-market sales (and being particularly successful with White House incumbents!). However, in the 1930s objectives became less grand, and so did the cars as the Lincoln Division had to develop its less-costly Zephyr line, and introduced Mercury as a rival to Oldsmobile.

Then in 1940 another prestige V12 model was introduced, largely as a result of the persistence of Edsel Ford, the Continental. It was true to the Lincoln traditions of the 1920s—large, costly and exclusive. It had sleek lines, in coupe or convertible styles (both, oddly, two-door bodies). Some body parts were common to Zephyrs, but the overall lines were not shared with other models after 1942 (the first cars, in 1940–41, had a Zephyr-style vee nose). When the Continental was re-introduced in 1946 the lines of the 1942 face lift were retained.

So were the car's mechanical features, notably the 75 degree side-valve V12, which had the seemingly modest capacity of 4,784 cc (292 cu in), and was rated at 120 bhp at 3,500 rpm. That was hardly adequate in a car that was substantially heavier than the Zephyr (which used the same engine); in an effort to overcome this the engine was bored out to 305 cu in in 1942, to gain 10 bhp. But in this form the engine was troublesome (off-centre bores were sometimes cast, resulting in cylinder walls that were too thin when machined) and in 1946 capacity reverted to 292 cu in, with revised gearing in an attempt to compensate, although Cadillac's push with new ohv V8s was difficult to counter with this V12.

Drive was through a three-speed manual gearbox, with a 'Columbia' two-speed axle (to be replaced with conventional overdrive in late cars). An automatic alternative was offered in 1942, but this 'Liquimatic' fluid coupling system was a failure, and the lack of an automatic option was to count against the Continental once freshly-designed rivals were marketed in the late 1940s. By that time the transverse-leaf suspension (beam axles front and rear) was archaic, too, but Henry Ford had stubbornly refused to follow GM's lead into independent front suspension.

Despite its shortcomings, the Continental continued to sell on its 'quality' virtues, particularly to the amount of genuine individual craftsmanship obviously put into each car. But even that was against the tide of automation, and so the Continental was increasingly a misfit. Nevertheless demand reached a new high in 1947, when 832 coupes and 738 cabriolets were sold; 1948 was to be the model's last year, but sales held up with 847 coupes and 452 cabriolets completed. The total production 1940–48 was 5,324 cars.

A Continental Mk II, with a 6,030 cc (368 cu in) 149 bhp V8 was introduced in 1956, with heavy publicity relying on the 'distinguished car that went before it'. But however well made, and however smooth its refined lines were, this Continental was an up-market badge-engineered Ford, and so was the Mk III that came in the 1960s. Neither was an exclusive car, neither had the distinction of a V12, neither was sufficiently 'different'. Despite its failings, such as mediocre performance, Edsel Ford's Lincoln Continental became a true American classic.

Overleaf and below: *The Lincoln Continental was a very imposing car, although the engineering was hardly advanced. This is a post-war example*

48
580 652
INDIANA

LOLA T70 MK III

1967–1969

In 1966 rumours began circulating that Aston Martin were planning a return to motor racing, and at the 1967 Racing Car Show Lola Cars displayed an elegant new sports coupe powered by an all new engine built by the Newport Pagnell-based firm.

The Lola Aston Martin, as the new machine was dubbed, was to be an all-British venture into international sports car racing, where Aston Martin had been so successful in the 1950s.

The car was a developed version of Lola's very successful open sports-racing T70, fitted with sleek enclosed glass-fibre bodywork and designated the T70 MkIII. The basis was a steel and aluminium monocoque chassis with two boxed side members housing the fuel tanks. Extremely strong front and rear bulkheads absorbed all suspension loads and provided a very rigid structure. Suspension was by the popular layout of double wishbones with coaxial coil spring/damper units, together with twin radius arms at the rear, for lateral and longitudinal location. Girling outboard disc brakes were used and a Hewland LG500 four-speed gearbox was fitted.

The experimental Aston Martin engine was an alloy 90 degree V8 unit, with twin overhead camshafts and a capacity of 5,064 cc (310 cu in). With the four twin-choke downdraught Weber carburettors fitted originally, a power output of 450 bhp at 6,500 rpm was anticipated. With fuel injection this was confidently expected to rise to 500 bhp. The two valve per cylinder engine weighed 238 kg (525 lb) less clutch.

The agreement with Aston Martin went up to the Le Mans 24 Hour race in June, but Lola founder and designer Eric Broadley intended to sell replicas, fitted with Chevrolet or Ford V8 engines, to private customers. Lola Racing was formed, comprising Lola Cars and Team Surtees, and 1964 World Champion John Surtees was to drive the lead car and supervise development of the Aston-engined cars.

Problems delayed the debut of the coupe, and it first appeared for the Le Mans Test Weekend in April. During these first really high speed runs the team encountered several snags. The engine (still running on carburettors) steadfastly refused to run above 6,000 rpm, and Surtees could not persuade the car above 296 km/h (185 mph), well below the target of 320 km/h (200 mph). Added to this the gear selection was initially baulky, the tail worked loose and one door blew off at speed. However, the car was third quickest overall, close behind the two works Ferraris and ahead of the Fords. It was quickest of all during the rainy second day.

With Lucas fuel injection the car next appeared at the Nürburgring 1,000 km, when in practice Surtees was second only to the 7-litre Chaparral 2F, and after a slow start was climbing through the field at an impressive rate when the rear suspension broke.

Two cars were prepared for Le Mans. It was a complete debacle. Surtees made an excellent start to run sixth on the opening lap, but at the end of lap three he pulled into the pits to retire with piston trouble after mere minutes of racing. Irwin fared

LOLA-ASTON MARTIN

Lola-Aston Martin

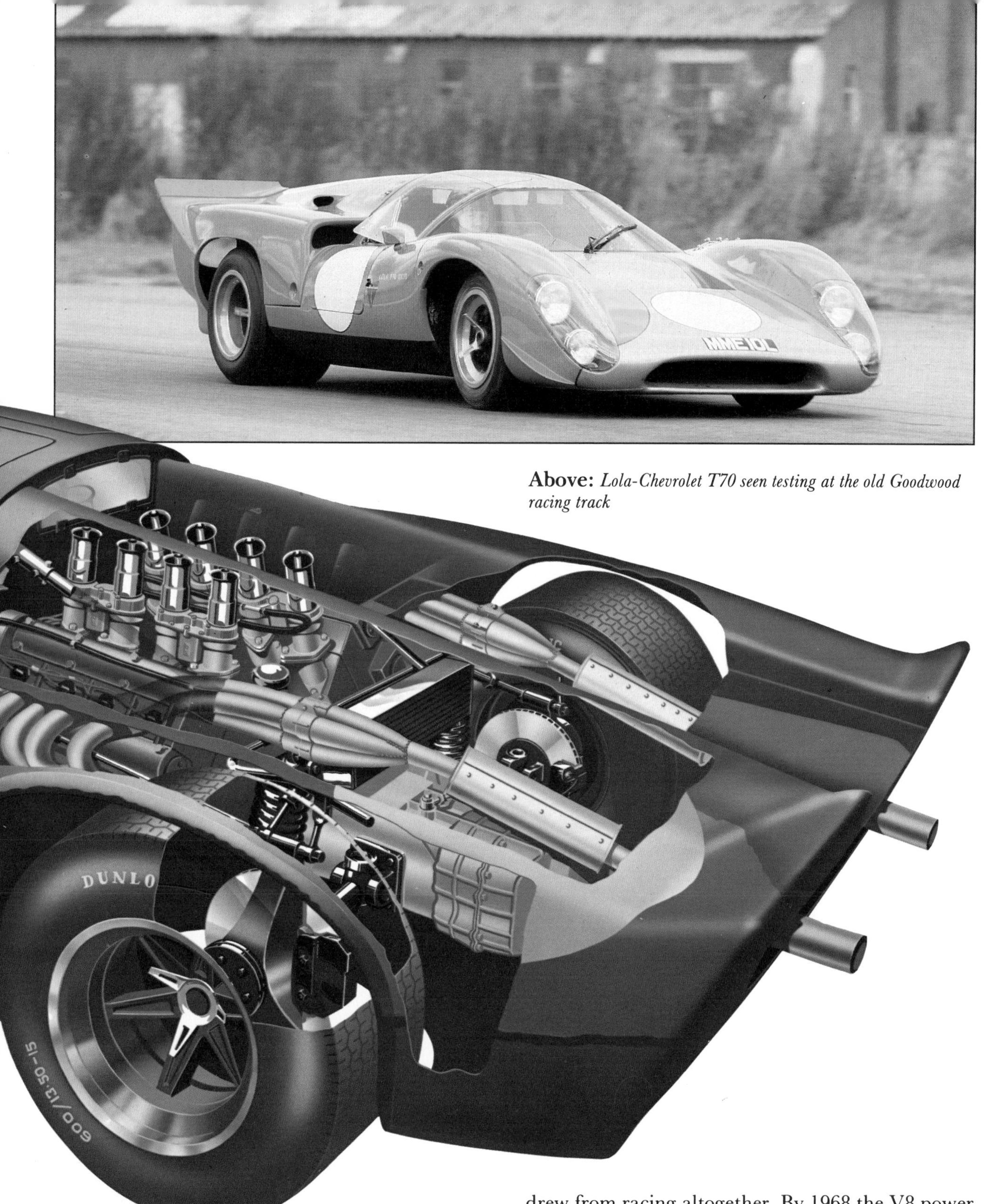

Above: *Lola-Chevrolet T70 seen testing at the old Goodwood racing track*

little better, pitting early with fuel pump maladies and retiring just after the 2½-hour mark with engine problems.

The cars never appeared again in international competition, although in the 1980s one appeared in historic events. Surtees, who had won the first CanAm championship in one of the original open T70s, ran Surtees Chevrolet-powered models with little success. Aston Martin concentrated on giving their engine the development it required and withdrew from racing altogether. By 1968 the V8 power unit was sufficiently refined for adoption as a road-going engine, and a development appeared in another abortive endurance racing car in the 1980s.

Lola pursued development of the T70, using Chevrolet engines, and in 1969 a Mk IIIb model won the Daytona 24 Hour race, with an older Mk III second. Generally, however, the T70 lacked stamina in long-distance races—in this respect the model would probably have benefitted from a development programme by a works team—although it was very successful in shorter 'sprint' races. More than 150 T70s were built, of which just over 100 were Mk IIIs.

LOTUS ELITE

1957–1963

One of the most unorthodox cars to appear in the late 1950s was the Lotus Elite, the first series production car designed by Colin Chapman, and the first intended principally as a road-going car.

Faced with the enormous costs of tooling-up for pressed steel body and chassis components, Chapman decided to make the integral chassis/body almost entirely from glass-reinforced plastics, breaking the structure down to three main mouldings, with the metal front suspension frame, the windscreen hoop and the engine and rear suspension mountings bonded in. The sleek body had a drag coefficient of only 0.29, and coupled with the car's low weight (680 kg) this contributed significantly to its performance.

In pursuance of his ideal of light weight allied to high performance, Chapman chose the famous aluminium alloy Coventry-Climax OHC engine of 1,216 cc (74 cu in), originally designed for use in a portable fire pump: the version produced for Lotus was a combination of the bore of the 1,460 cc and the stroke of the 1,098 cc units.

In standard form, with a single 1.5 in SU carburettor, the FWE developed a modest 75 bhp; twin carburettors boosted this 85 bhp, and ultimately the unremarkable engine was developed to produce more than 100 bhp without losing reliability.

The Elite was first announced at the 1957 London Motor Show, and its revolutionary construction method was not the only notable feature of the car: it also boasted independent suspension and disc brakes all round (inboard at the rear). The latter feature caused some of the few teething problems with the body structure, as the heat generated by the rear brakes was responsible for the failure of the mountings that carried the differential unit. The body structure also proved noisy, and this was a major drawback in cars built up by amateurs from kits (in common with minor British companies, Lotus sold cars in 'kit' form in the 1950s).

Like the later Lotus-Ford GP car, the Elite was an immediate competitions success, winning at Silverstone in 1958 and taking a class victory at Le Mans in 1959. Further class victories were won every year from 1960 to 1964. The Elite was successful in many events—hardly surprising, for it really was a race-developed car, the suspension, steering and brakes all having been proved in the 1957 Lotus Formula 2 car.

In its ultimate road form, the car was capable of nearly 193 km/h (120 mph) coupled with fuel consumption of only 6.44 litres/100 km (43.75 mpg) as a steady 129 km/h (80 mph). Only 988 examples of this outstanding car were built before production ended in 1963, for the enormous production and marketing problems it posed for the small Lotus company were never fully overcome.

LOTUS ESPRIT

1975 ONWARD

In the early 1970s Colin Chapman decided to shift the emphasis of the Lotus road car range up-market: in 1975 the Esprit became the supercar flagship, setting high standards of performance with normal and turbocharged engines.

The Esprit was the last of a batch of new models to be introduced, following the front-engined Elite and Eclat which had appeared a year earlier. Like them, it was powered by the Lotus 907 slant-four engine, a dohc 16-valve unit which in its first 1,973 cc (120 cu in) form produced 160 bhp at 6,200 rpm. In the Esprit it was mounted behind the cockpit, canted at 45 degrees to the left, and it drove through a Citroen SM-based five-speed gearbox which allowed for positive and reasonably quick changes. In this form the Esprit had a maximum speed of 130 mph (210 kmh). More was to come with more power, putting the car into a performance class appropriate to its chassis, running gear and brakes.

The backbone-cum-space frame chassis was clothed in elegant glass-fibre-reinforced bodywork following lines first seen on a show car by the Italian stylist Giugiaro in 1972. It had a pronounced wedge profile — the nose fell away very sharply — and accommodation for two. In comfort terms there were shortcomings, for tall people especially, and in other respects such as visibility and ventilation. Suspension was independent all round, and gave a comfortable ride as well as outstanding roadholding and handling. In those aspects it was so far in advance of most of its contemporaries that it seemed almost ironical that in the early 1980s Lotus should use it as a test vehicle for their 'active suspension' system, aimed at achieving improvements in ride, roadholding and handling!

Early in 1980 the Esprit Turbo was announced, at a lavish function arranged by the Lotus Grand Prix team sponsor, Essex, whose brash colours the first cars wore. For this car the 907-based 910 engine in 2,174 cc (132 cu in) form was fitted with a Garrett AiResearch T3 turbocharger, while appropriate internal modifications were aimed to strengthen and ensure reliability. The power output went up to 210 bhp at 6,500 rom, and the maximum speed to over 245 kmh (152 mph). This model was by no means an Esprit with a turbo pack bolted to the engine, for a considerable complementary development programme led to substantial revisions.

The same year saw the introduction of the Series 2.2 model, with a normally-aspirated 910 engine, rated at 160 bhp, and in 1981 the chassis and suspension of the Turbo were adopted for the Series 3 Esprit (with relatively small production runs, any rationalization was welcome). Maximum speed of the Series 3 car was 220 kmh (138 mph), with excellent fuel consumption figures recorded by the official system, for example 8.5 litres/100 km (33.3 mpg) at a constant 75 mph, compared with the 11.7 litres/100 km (24.9 mpg) returned by the Turbo Esprit. Coupled with scintillating acceleration, figures like this confirm the technical and aerodynamic excellence of the last Lotus road model wholly designed under the direction of Colin Chapman.

MASERATI 3500GT

1957–1964

In the mid-1950s, Count Adolfo Orsi recognized the need to redirect his Maserati company, away from the racing that had brought it close to ruin, and to move it well up-market. The result was the 3500GT.

The starting point was the 350S engine, then the largest power unit from Maserati's racing cars. Designer Alfieri turned this into a production engine of 3,485 cc (211 cu in) for installation in a new, larger, chassis. The engine was a classic twin-ohc straight-six. There were only two valves per cylinder, but two spark plugs fired the mixture in each of the cylinder head combustion chambers. Initially, the unit gave a claimed 230 bhp at 5,500 rpm on a compression ratio of 8.2:1.

The new chassis into which the engine was installed was a simple ladder-frame with sheet steel stiffening. Suspension was by double wishbones at the front, with a leaf-sprung live rear axle, the latter having an anti-roll bar to balance the handling characteristics. Drive was taken from the engine through a dry-plate clutch and a ZF four-speed gearbox. Unusually for a car of this performance, drum brakes were fitted all round to the early models, and many drivers considered that they were not sufficient to stop the car in adequate time from the claimed top speed of 230 km/h (142 mph).

First shown publicly at the 1957 Geneva Motor Show, the car was built in relatively large numbers until 1964, when it was effectively replaced by the Mistral. The two main production versions were the coupé by Touring of Milan, and the open Spider by Vignale. No fewer than 1,975 of the Touring cars were built, although the Spider is rarer, only 242 being constructed. Further small batches of cars or 'one-offs' were built to special order by coachbuilders such as Allemano, Bertone and Frua.

As production proceeded, various changes were made to the specification. In 1959, Alfieri undertook a major engine re-design to ease production problems and to improve the refinement of the unit: after this, the output rose to 260 bhp. In 1962, Lucas fuel injection was offered as an alternative to the triple-Weber carburettor arrangement, and cars thus equipped were known as 3500GTIs. A five-speed gearbox with an overdrive top was also offered in place of the original four-speed unit.

Disc front brakes were adopted in 1960, overcoming the worst faults of the all-drum system and eventually, the late-series cars were equipped with disc brakes all round. The chassis itself was never substantially changed and was in fact carried over to the Mistral, 'cart-sprung' live rear axle and all. The relative crudeness of the chassis meant that the car had to be driven with respect, especially in the wet. This was all the more pertinent, as the 3500GT was undoubtedly fast, though acceleration and the maximum speed depended greatly on the overall gearing (Maserati offered three alternative final drives, one lower and two higher, for their standard 3.77:1 rear axle).

The 3500GT gained a considerable reputation, and most of the cars produced were equipped to a very high standard, even to the point of having some of the earliest electrically operated windows seen in Europe, and a standard heating and ventilation system that was as complicated as it was effective, its explanation in the handbook taking up four pages.

MERCEDES 300SL

1954–1963

The foundation of Mercedes-Benz' all-conquering return to Grand Prix racing in 1954 had been laid two years before with a streamlined sports-racing car that became a legend: the 300SL.

Light it was, with an aluminium body surrounding a tubular spaceframe chassis carrying coil spring and wishbone front suspension and low-pivot swinging axles at the rear. Its overhead camshaft 2,996 cc (183 cu in) six-cylinder engine, developed from that of the 300S, was inclined in the frame at 45 degrees to the left to give an unusually low bonnet line and to minimize the frontal area.

In its racing debut, the model took second and fourth places in the gruelling Mille Miglia, driven by Karl Kling and Rudolph Caracciola respectively, and then won the other four races that it was entered for, including Le Mans.

Capitalizing on the success of the car, Mercedes-Benz launched a limited production road-going version of the 300SL in 1954, which made most rival supercars of the time look decidedly pedestrian. It retained the racer's basic design and several of its more unusual features, including a folding steering wheel to facilitate entry through gullwing doors that were themselves necessitated by waist-high frame members that gave the chassis its great rigidity.

Although it weighed over 1,280 kg (2,800 lb), more than the racing version, the production 300SL was more powerful. Using Bosch direct fuel injection and a higher 8.55:1 compression ratio, output was raised to 215 bhp at 5,800 rpm. With the highest (3.25:1) of several alternative final drive ratios, the car had a claimed top speed of 260 km/h (160 mph), though contemporary reports indicated that this may have been a little optimistic unless the car was specially tuned. With the lower axle ratios, top speed was sacrificed for incredible acceleration, with a time of only 7 seconds from rest to 100 km/h (60 mph). Even by today's standards, these are remarkable figures: in 1955, they were sensational.

The closed coupe was replaced in 1957 by an open roadster, a real wind-in-the-hair sports car better equipped than the gullwing for everyday use, and, to offset its greater weight, even more powerful. Raising the compression ratio to 9.5:1 and using a higher-lift camshaft increased output to around 225 bhp (the often-quoted 250 bhp is a somewhat misleading gross figure). The roadster's modified spaceframe, constructed of heavier gauge tubing to compensate for its shallower side-members, allowed the use of conventional doors, although purists mourned the demise of the classic gullwing version which is still the more prized—and the rarer—of the two. Massive finned drum brakes were retained on the roadster long after disc brakes, finally adopted by Mercedes-Benz in 1961, had become commonplace on other high-performance cars.

If the 300SL had a weakness, it lay not in the brakes but in the rear suspension design. The introduction on the roadster of an ingenious transverse compensating spring linking the two half axle-shafts to increase bump stiffness but not resistance to roll—a layout later adopted on other Mercedes-Benz models—minimized the unpleasant effects of rear wheel camber changes. Even so, the swinging rear axles of the 300SL in both its forms gave the car a reputation of being tricky to handle on the limit of adhesion.

In all, over 3,000 300SLs were made—1,400 gullwings (1954–1957) and 1,858 roadsters (1957–1963). Cherished and revered as one of the all-time supercar classics, most are still in existence and now valued very highly.

Best recalled in its 'Gullwing' form **(following pages),** *the Mercedes-Benz 300SL was one of the sensational cars of the 1950s. The 300SL Roadster* **(left)** *succeeded the Gullwing in 1957*

MERCEDES-BENZ 600

1963–1981

The huge and luxurious Mercedes-Benz 600 was conceived quite simply as a flagship for the Mercedes range and examples have been used by politicians, pop stars and millionaires the world over.

Known also as the "Grosser" Mercedes, the 600 of 1963 finally went out of production in 1981 after some 2,677 had been made. Following the fuel crisis of the early 1970s it became available to order only, as even the super rich seemed by that date to be worrying about fuel consumption and the high cost of the 600. However, many examples are still in service around the world, cropping up on state occasions, or international events when a dignitary wants to cut a dash by appearing in a car other than a Rolls Royce, but one that is just as prestigious.

Everything about the 600 was 'big' right from the start. Replete with giant steel monocoque, the car weighed in at 2½ tons, yet its 250 bhp 6.3-litre engine made it capable of cruising at speeds in excess of 195 km/h (120 mph). In fact the 600 was the first Mercedes-Benz to use a V8 engine and it was this powerful unit from the 600 that found its way into both the 300 SEL 6.3 saloon and latterly the 450 SEL in bored out(!) 6.9-litre form. Perhaps understandably, both these cars are exceptionally fast.

The V8 engine has its banks of cylinders at 90°. The block is cast iron but the heads are light alloy with one camshaft each. Bosch fuel injection came as standard. A column-controlled auto gearbox was fitted to all examples on the assumption that most would be chauffeur-driven. It was for this reason too that a sliding glass partition was inserted between the front and rear seats so that high finance or superstardom could be discussed in privacy.

The suspension system that the Mercedes engineers devised for the new car was truly mind-boggling, with high-pressure pneumatic suspension units all round. There were additional rubber springs, telescopic dampers and, to cap it all, a self-levelling control system for the rear. This ensured that the car's occupants were whisked along in maximum comfort while the sumptuous trim and ample soundproofing meant that very little road noise reached them in the cabin.

Naturally everything about the car was power-assisted, from the steering and brakes to the windows and door locks; commonplace now but unusual in 1963. The body style of the 600 could hardly be described as elegant or sleek but it is certainly very imposing. If the standard 5.5 m (18 ft) version wasn't enough for you, there was also the option of the long-wheelbase version known as the Pullman, which Mercedes' stylists managed to make 6.2 m (20.5 ft) long, offering the extraordinary option of six doors rather than the normal four. Of course, a handful of 600 customers went even further than this and had their 600s fitted with a semi-convertible body for public appearances. In these days of security worries for international figures one suspects that these open versions will have been discarded in favour of bullet-proofed variants.

The 600 was not really developed during its 18-year production run and its once-modern design soon seemed old-fashioned especially when considerd against the progress made by Mercedes with their smaller cars. The "Grosser" Mercedes may no longer be made, but the great strength and engineering quality of those that were built should ensure that they remain in existence for many years yet.

M.G. TC MIDGET

1945–1949

Asked to name a sports car, many people would still say 'M.G.', and a large number of those would probably have the M.G. TC in mind. Clarke Gable, Phil Hill, Briggs Cunningham, the young Philip Mountbatten who took the future Queen of England out for drives in one—these were among the 10,000 who bought and fell in love with Abingdon's first post-war two-seater.

Of that number, 66 per cent went overseas, which was a considerable mystery to all concerned in the motor industry because even at that time, the design was out of date by any standards. The TC was not available with left-hand drive, it had no heater or radio, and had very little luggage space; its non-independent suspension gave an exceptionally uncomfortable ride, the steering was peculiar when new and diabolical when old, and in standard form, this so-called sports car was not even particularly fast.

In fact the basic design was already ten years old when the TC went into full production, dating back to the TA of 1936. There was a simple box-section chassis and semi-elliptic leaf springs at the front and rear, hydraulic dampers and hydraulic brakes. The body looked strangely anachronistic, its angularity emphasized by the fold-flat windscreen, separate headlamps and sidelamps, and even a separate fuel tank which was fixed by metal straps to the square tail behind the spare wheel mounting.

The 1,250 cc (76 cu in) four-cylinder engine had pushrod OHV, and although shorter in stroke than the old TA unit, it was still so long compared to its bore size that it should have been (but was not) unreliable. Untuned, it gave a modest 54.4 bhp at 5,200 rpm, but fortunately the whole car weighed little more than 762 kg (1,650 lb), so the TC could accelerate from 0 to 100 km/h (0 to 60 mph) in just over 21 seconds, and it had a maximum speed of 120 km/h (75 mph) even on the low-grade petrol then available in the UK. This meant that it had an acceptable turn of performance by the standards of its day A lengthy and worldwide score of competition successes at club level confirms that the TC engine responded well to tuning, and could readily be persuaded to give over 80 bhp. And in accordance with Abingdon's policy, the TC's handling was as trustworthy as its engine.

The days have long passed when a TC could be bought cheaply. Almost anywhere in the world it is now revered as a classic sports car. There is today little hope of finding an example that is original, unrestored, and in decent condition. Fortunately, there are many sources of spares, especially in the USA, and most components have been reproduced.

A sadly-decayed M.G. TC is likely to cost rather more than a less popular car in better condition, but it is such a simple design that the final cost after restoration may not be all that much higher. And an M.G. TC is fun to drive in its own special way—which was the secret of its success in the first place.

Below: *Standard M.G. TC.* **Overleaf:** *Typical competition-modified TC*

M.G. MAGNETTE ZA/ZB

1953–1958

As the very last Abingdon-built M.G. saloon, the ZA/ZB Magnette also marked a turning point, for it was a model using components from other BMC cars.

Due to a widespread, but quite mistaken notion that all previous Magnettes had been sports or racing models, some of those who saw the saloon at the 1953 London Motor Show denounced it as both effeminate and Italianate, despite the fact that the styling was the work of the Jowett Javelin's designer, Gerald Palmer. Early criticism soon gave way, however, to the view of many, that this was the most handsome four-door saloon that M.G. ever made. It succeeded the Y models, which used many Morris body pressings.

Palmer combined his body, originally designed for M.G., but previously used for the Wolseley 4/44 with the British Motor Corporation's new 1,489 cc (91 cu in) pushrod OHV four-cylinder engine, a choice that meant the Wolseley version of the car had an M.G. engine (the old 1,250 cc T-type in a detuned state), whereas the M.G. version had an Austin-based unit derived from the original post-war A40!

The new Magnette soon showed its paces in international rallies and production-car racing, and within two years of the launch, M.G. were building six ZA saloons at Abingdon for every TF two-seater to satisfy the demand. By then, the new engine had also been seen at Le Mans, under the bonnets of the prototype MGA team cars in 1955. At the 1956 London Motor Show, BMC announced the ZB, which had 68 bhp as opposed to the 60 bhp output of the ZA engine: the increase was derived from a higher compression ratio, double valve springs and bigger SU carburettors, plus tougher big-end bearings and full-flow filtration. The final drive ratio was raised from 4.8756:1 to 4.55:1 at the same time. Body changes included a full-width parcel shelf and a dished steering wheel, with straight chrome flashes on the front wings instead of the earlier curved 'hockey sticks'. An option, known as the 'ZB Varitone' had two-colour paintwork, a chrome waistline and a wraparound rear window.

Despite compact dimensions—the car was 429 cm (14 ft 1 in) long overall, and 160 cm (5 ft 3in) wide, with a wheelbase of 259 cm (8 ft 6 in)—the Magnette scaled 1,118 kg (2,464 lb). A sturdily built vehicle, it had such luxury touches as thick carpeting, hefty leather seats and plenty of polished woodwork. So although it felt outstandingly taut and rattle-free to drive, with precise rack-and-pinion steering and firm suspension giving good roadholding, the power-to-weight ratio was rather poor. An untuned ZA could just achieve 130 km/h (80 mph), and a ZB 145 km/h (90 mph), but the time taken to reach 100 km/h (60 mph) was 23 and 18.5 seconds respectively. Fuel consumption was fairly heavy at around 11.3 litres/100 km (25 mpg).

In December 1958, the ZB was dropped in favour of the Cowley-built Farina-designed Magnette Mark III. In all, 12,754 ZAs and 23,846 ZBs were built.

M.G. MGA
1955–1962

The MGA succeeded the last of the 'T' models in 1955, inheriting only the front suspension from the TF, and it did much to restore the marque's sporting reputation.

It was the first M.G. sports car to have full-width bodywork, which was mounted on a substantial separate chassis. BMC B-series mechanical components used included the 1,489 cc (91 cu in) engine, which was rated at 68 bhp when the model was introduced and was uprated to give 72 bhp in 1956.

In this form the MGA had a top speed marginally below the magic 100 mph (160 km/h). To achieve this, the engine capacity was increased to 1,588 cc (97 cu in) in 1959 for the 1600, and output to 75 bhp; for the 1600 Mk II in 1960 the engine was bored out to 1,622 cc (99 cu in), and the MGA in standard form at last became a genuine 100 mph car. Meanwhile twin overhead camshaft variants of the engine had appeared, in the EX179 record car, which exceeded 275 km/h (170 mph) at Utah in 1956, then in supercharged form in the mid-engined EX181 projectile which Stirling Moss drove to exceed 395 km/h (245 mph). Eventually a twin ohc engine was introduced in a production road car, the MGA Twin Cam, announced in July 1958.

This had centrelock steel wheels, disc brakes all round, and a far more potent engine. The maximum speed had been raised from 160 to 185 km/h (100 to 115 mph). Roadholding characteristics were similar to those of the 1500: cornered hard, the tail would slide quite early, but completely under control, making it great fun to drive along twisty roads.

The original engine was increased to 1,588 cc (97 cu in) by enlarging the bores. Service checks were difficult because of the sheer size of the new cylinder head, which cut down accessibility for other maintenance jobs. SU H6 carburettors, fitted in place of the H4 units on the 1500, combined with a massive increase in compression ratio, helped to raise the power output to 108 bhp. It was a noisy engine, and tended to burn a lot of oil, while the 9.9:1 compression ratio made 100-octane fuel essential.

Combustion chamber temperatures soared if the ignition timing was over-advanced or if the mixture was set too lean so these settings were highly critical, and even when they were correct, a careless driver could destroy the engine simply by over-revving so that the valves met the piston crowns. Because of continual service problems, the Twin Cam was discontinued in April 1960 after 2,111 cars had been built, of which a mere 360 were sold in the UK.

Twin Cam MGAs had a modestly successful racing career, winning their class in the *Autosport* Sports Car Championship in 1959 and 1960, and twice took a class third in the Tourist Trophy Race (1968 and 1960). They scored a class 1-2-3 in the 1959 Silverstone GT Race, came second and third at last year's Sebring 12 Hours, and in 1960 won the 2-litre class at Le Mans, averaging 146.7 km/h (91.12 mph) overall for the 24 hours.

The original MGA 1500 was in production until 1959, and production reached 58,750; the MGA 1600 ran until 1962, 40,220 being built before it was superseded by the MGB.

M.G. MGA Twin Cam roadster

MINI-COOPER

1961–1971

Announced in September 1961, the Mini-Cooper became one of the most successful competition saloons ever devised, with a seemingly endless record of wins in international rallies and saloon car races.

These include the Tulip, the Finnish and the Circuit of Ireland rallies three times a piece, the Three Cities, Polish and Czechoslovakian events twice each, and the Tour de France, RAC, Swedish, and Geneva rallies, together with the European Rally Championship and the Saloon Racing Championship. This fine record of successes, achieved mainly during the golden years of BMC's Competitions Department from 1962 to 1967, does not include the Monte Carlo Rally, the Mini-Cooper won outright three times, and some say four (it was disqualified in its first outing on dubious grounds).

By 1964, the Monte Carlo Rally had lost much of its amateur character, and, as more works teams entered, the private individuals tended to drop out because they could not compete with the resources of the team cars. The Mini-Coopers proved beyond all doubt that the right car, properly prepared, could sweep the board; in 1964, Paddy Hopkirk won, and his victory was repeated by Timo Makinen in 1965. In 1966, Mini-Coopers took the first four places in the rally, but were then disqualified on a tiny detail of the headlight dipping arrangements: this promoted the French Citroen driven by Toivonen to victory, but the next year, the superiority of the Mini-Cooper was underlined when Rauno Aaltonen won the event, after a close tussle with the Lancia of Ove Andersson.

The first Mini-Cooper had a long-stroke 997 cc (61 cu in) engine with a modified camshaft and cylinder head to differentiate it from the standard Mini. Larger valves and ports, a compression ratio of 9:1 and twin 1¼ in SU carburettors boosted the power output to 55 bhp and gave a top speed of 137 km/h (85 mph), which was a good 16 km/h (10 mph) faster than the standard 34 bhp Mini 850. In March 1964, the engine was changed for a short-stroke 998 cc unit, which gave the same power at lower rpm and an improved torque curve, which increased performance all round.

The first Mini-Cooper S, which was designed to be an even faster version of the car that John Cooper, the racing team manager, had suggested to Sir George Harriman, the BMC chairman, appeared in 1963. It featured a short-stroke 1,071 cc (65 cu in) engine with an entirely different block which had offset bores and con rods, a nitrided big-journal crankshaft, forged rockers, stellited Nimonic valves, bonded clutch linings, and thicker front brake discs with bigger pads and servo-assisted operation to match the increase in power (now 70 bhp at 6,200 rpm). With the optional 3.44:1 final drive unit, 153 km/h (95 mph) was possible.

In the next year, two more S models were announced: the rare 65 bhp (59 cu in) short-stroke 970 cc racer, and the more familiar 1,275 cc (78 cu in) version, which gave 75 bhp at only 5,800 rpm and more low-speed torque, so that mid-range acceleration was noticeably improved, although the top speed was little improved.

In total, 100,051 Mini-Coopers were built between 1961 and 1969, of which 67 per cent were exported, 45,442 Mini-Cooper S models (1963–71), of which 79 per cent were exported, and a further 583 S models were actually built overseas in 1973.

MORGAN PLUS-4 SUPER SPORTS

1962–1968

The introduction of the Plus 4 Super Sports, extended the Malvern Link firm's reputation for producing genuine sports cars.

The Plus 4 was originally launched in 1950, first fitted with the Standard Vanguard engine of 2,088 cc (127 cu in) capacity, and later with the linered-down Triumph TR2 version of this engine in 1954 and the TR3 unit in 1956. In true Morgan fashion, sliding pillar front suspension was used, a system that had been tried early in the century by the founder, H. F. S. Morgan, and has been retained ever since.

The Super Sports was born during the 1959 Six-hour Relay race at Silverstone, in which Chris Lawrence entered and raced his Plus 4.

From 1960, customers could request a Lawrence-tuned engine to be fitted to their Plus 4s, and in almost every case, the car was fitted with lightweight aluminium body panels. In1962, the Super Sports was officially launched as a model in its own right, and this proved to be a fitting successor to a long line of Morgan sporting thoroughbreds.

The Super Sports was basically a 4/4 body fitted to a Plus 4 chassis; aluminium alloy panels were fitted as standard and further changes from the standard Plus 4 specification included the fitment of a raked radiator and header tank (made necessary because of the lower 4/4 shaped body), and the incorporation of a flare in the bonnet to permit the use of twin Weber DCOE8 carburettors. Externally, therefore, there were only subtle differences from the standard model; under the bonnet, however, was a very different matter.

The TR3 power unit was of 1,991 cc (121 cu in) capacity, and for the Super Sports it was re-built with a fully balanced crankshaft and fly-wheel, polished and balanced pistons and con-rods, a polished and gas-flowed cylinder head and manifolds, a four-branch exhaust, special camshaft, an oil cooler, and the twin Weber carburettors and radiator header tank mentioned above. On a compression ratio of 9:1, the unit produced 115 bhp at 5,500 rpm, giving a top speed of around 195 km/h (120 mph). Later, the TR4 engine was fitted, and the increased capacity of 2,138 cc (130 cu in) raised the performance still further.

The Super Sports soon showed its worth in competition. In 1960, Lawrence broke Porsche's 2-litre lap record at the Nürburgring 1,000 km race, and the organizers awarded him a special prize for a car 'that only seemed to spend a quarter of the race on the ground'. Two years later, Lawrence and Shepherd-Barron took the 2-litre GT class at Le Mans, and other successes included a 1-2-3 class win at the Grand Prix de Spa in 1963. The Super Sports won numerous races at a secondary level.

Production ceased in 1968, just before the introduction of the V8-engined Plus 8.

TOK 258. The famous first Super Sports Morgan

MORRIS MINOR

1948–1971

Designed by Alec Issigonis, who went on to design the Mini, the Morris Minor had enormous popularity, a production life of 22 years and an appeal almost as enduring as the Ford Model T or Volkswagen 'Beetle'.

The Morris Minor was introduced towards the end of 1948 and was greeted with enthusiasm by a car-hungry world. Launched as a replacement for the successful Morris Eights, the new Minor was hailed as a small car that was comfortable, economical and as quick as considerably larger and more expensive vehicles of the late 1940s. This reputation was to continue through several developments, mainly small design changes and increases in engine size and performance, until 1971 when the car was discontinued in favour of the BL Marina.

The first model had a 918 cc (55 cu in) side-valve engine which gave a top speed of 98 kmh (61 mph) and a 0–30 mph acceleration time of 12.3 seconds — not fast but a useful cruising ability. The car was distinctive with its headlights in the front grill and wide, solid appearance. It could hold four people comfortably and had an average fuel consumption of 7 litres/100 km (40 mpg). In 1950 a tourer was announced, aimed principally at the American market, and it was US lighting regulations that forced in 1951 the first and only major change to the body design: the headlights were moved from the front grill to the side wings. Along with this the BMC 'A' series 803 cc (49 cu in) ohv engine was adopted, which with its output of 30 bhp gave a small increase in top speed. At the same time a new model was added to the range: the 'timber-framed' estate version known as the Traveller.

The first real development occurred in 1956 with the introduction of the Minor 1000, considered by many to be the most typical Morris Minor. Included in the package was a new 948 cc (57 cu in) ohv engine rated at 37 bhp which boosted overall acceleration and gave a top speed of 117 kmh (73 mph), as well as design changes like the introduction of a one-piece windscreen. From this time on there was little change in the body shape but in 1964 there was another increase in engine size, this time to 1,098 cc (67 cu in) which gave better acceleration but little change to top speed.

When production ceased in 1971 over 1.6 million Morris Minors had been produced, many of them going to all parts of the world as vital British post-war exports. This little car is now accepted as a classic of it type and a enduring testament to its solid construction and reliability is the number of examples that are still in use today, many of them still as every day transport.

1949 Morris Minor. Popular and endearing

NSU RO80

1967–1977

Unhesitatingly given the accolade of Car of the Year by a group of the most influential European motoring journalists after its appearance in 1967, the NSU Ro80 was later dubbed by some the Car of the Decade.

It seemed to deserve all the plaudits it won, but in the long run it was not a success. It was not the first production car to feature a Wankel rotary engine—NSU earned that distinction earlier with their little Wankel Spyder, a very short (and prearranged) time ahead of the Mazda 110. However, it was the first car to be designed around the Wankel engine in such a way that it could not have been the same car with any other power unit.

NSU recognized that the Ro80 would be of crucial importance in establishing a favourable public attitude to later Wankel-engined products, and were generous in making the car to a high standard of quality. The power steering, for example, was exceptionally good by the standards of the time, possibly the best there was. The drag coefficient was inferior only to the Citroen in its class and the silence, roadholding, comfort of ride and luxury of the interior, all stood comparison with cars recognised as being among the best.

With its twin-chamber Wankel engine capable of producing 113 bhp at 5,500 rpm and 16.1 kg/m (117 lb ft) of torque at 4,500 rpm, it was necessary for the transmission to embody a fluid coupling, so NSU combined a torque converter coupling with an automatic clutch and a three-speed synchromesh gearbox, enabling the driver to enjoy full control of the transmission while being free to use his left foot on the brake as there was no clutch pedal. Driven skilfully, the Ro80 was a lively car, and with its soft, long-travel all-independent suspension (MacPherson struts in front, trailing wishbones aft) and disc brakes on all four wheels, it was capable of maintaining very high average speeds on all manner of roads.

Alas, it suffered abuse from early owners. Some of them over-revved it mercilessly (inducing converter-coupling distortion) for the engine would run up to 9,000 rpm if asked, though it was red-lined at 6,500. Other drivers slogged away at low speeds in town. Neither habit was good for the car, which needed years of development to overcome sealing problems, bore wear, and spark plug troubles. While the car as a whole had been well conceived and executed by chief engineer Praxl's team, development chief Froede had a very hard time making the engine as good as the rest of the car. By 1974, everything reasonable and necessary had been done, but then the oil crisis struck, and suddenly the Wankel engine, whose emissions had been the object of much biased criticism and much gifted engineering, was promptly dismissed as a fuel guzzler. In its original form it never was, being capable of a respectable 13.5 litres/100 km (21 mpg), but the cleansing of its exhaust had cost it dear in fuel consumption. The weight of luxury did not help: the car weighed 1,382 kg (3,045 lb).

NSU never recovered from the fuel crisis, and neither did the car. In the early 1980s the only Wankel-engined cars came from Japan, but the good that the Ro80 could have done was undermined by many factors beyond NSU's control. In its 10 year production life, just 37,204 Ro80s were built. Some have since been fitted with Ford V4 engine by owners who felt that reliability was more important than the smooth sophistication of the rather temperamental rotary but many other owners feel that this is to take a retrograde step.

NISSAN 300ZX

1984 ONWARD

Ever since Datsun introduced the 240Z sports car back in 1971, subsequent models in the 'Z car' range have all earned a cult following, and some deservedly have become the world's best-selling sports cars.

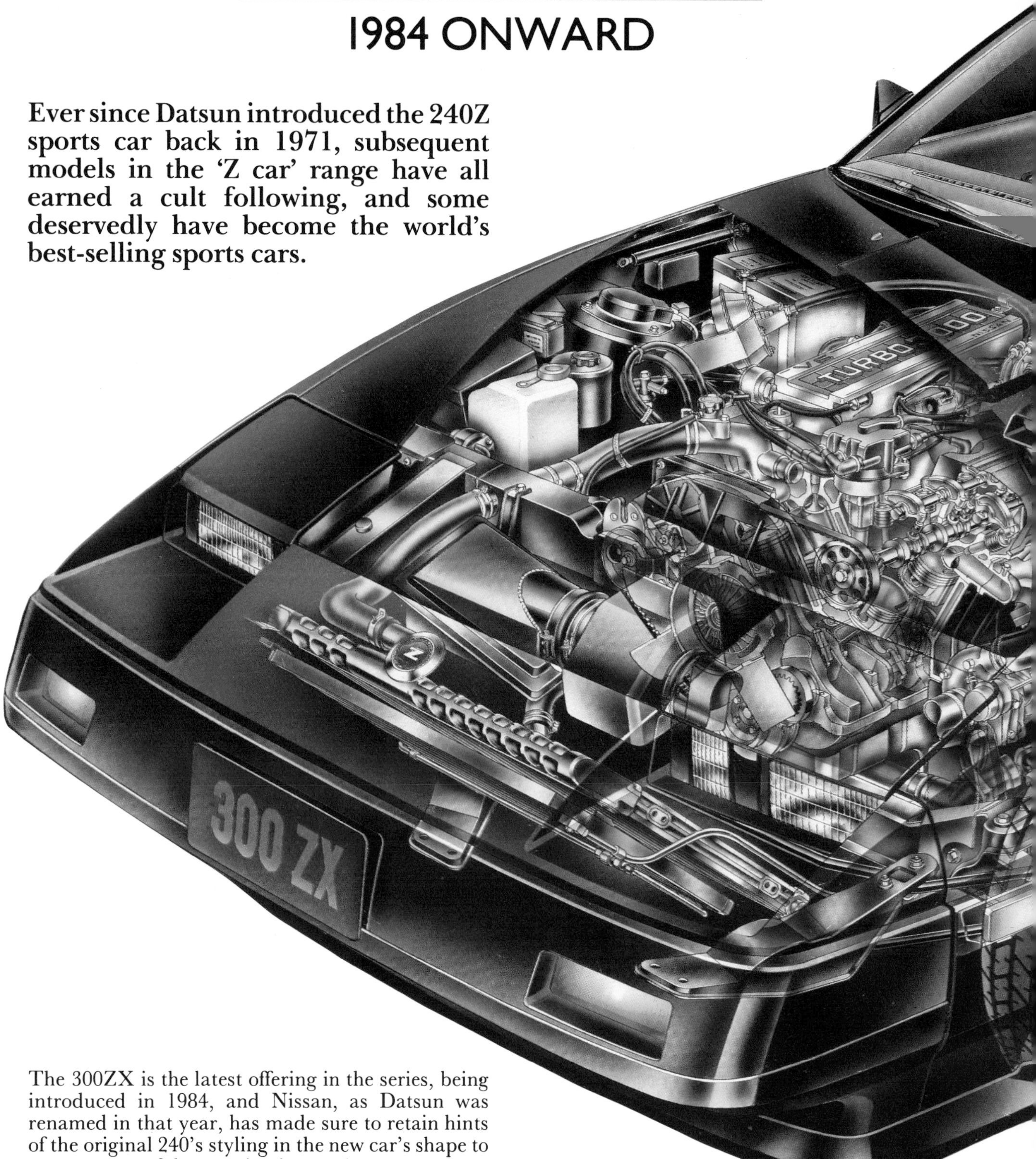

The 300ZX is the latest offering in the series, being introduced in 1984, and Nissan, as Datsun was renamed in that year, has made sure to retain hints of the original 240's styling in the new car's shape to restore some of the sporting image that was perhaps lost with the 300ZX's somewhat lacklustre predecessor, the 280ZX.

Replacing the 280's rather lazy straight-six engine with a new 2,960 cc (180 cu in) V6 with single overhead camshafts, Nissan have put the 300ZX firmly in the lower reaches of the supercar league. With 170 bhp (DIN) on tap the car is certainly no sluggard, but the addition of a turbocharger bumps the power output up to a hefty 228 bhp (DIN) at 5,400 rpm giving the 300ZX Turbo a claimed top speed of 240 km/h (150 mph) with the 0–60 mph dash coming up in a shade under 7 seconds — and that's enough to see off such cars as the Porsche 944 and Lotus Excel, the 300ZX's most obvious rivals.

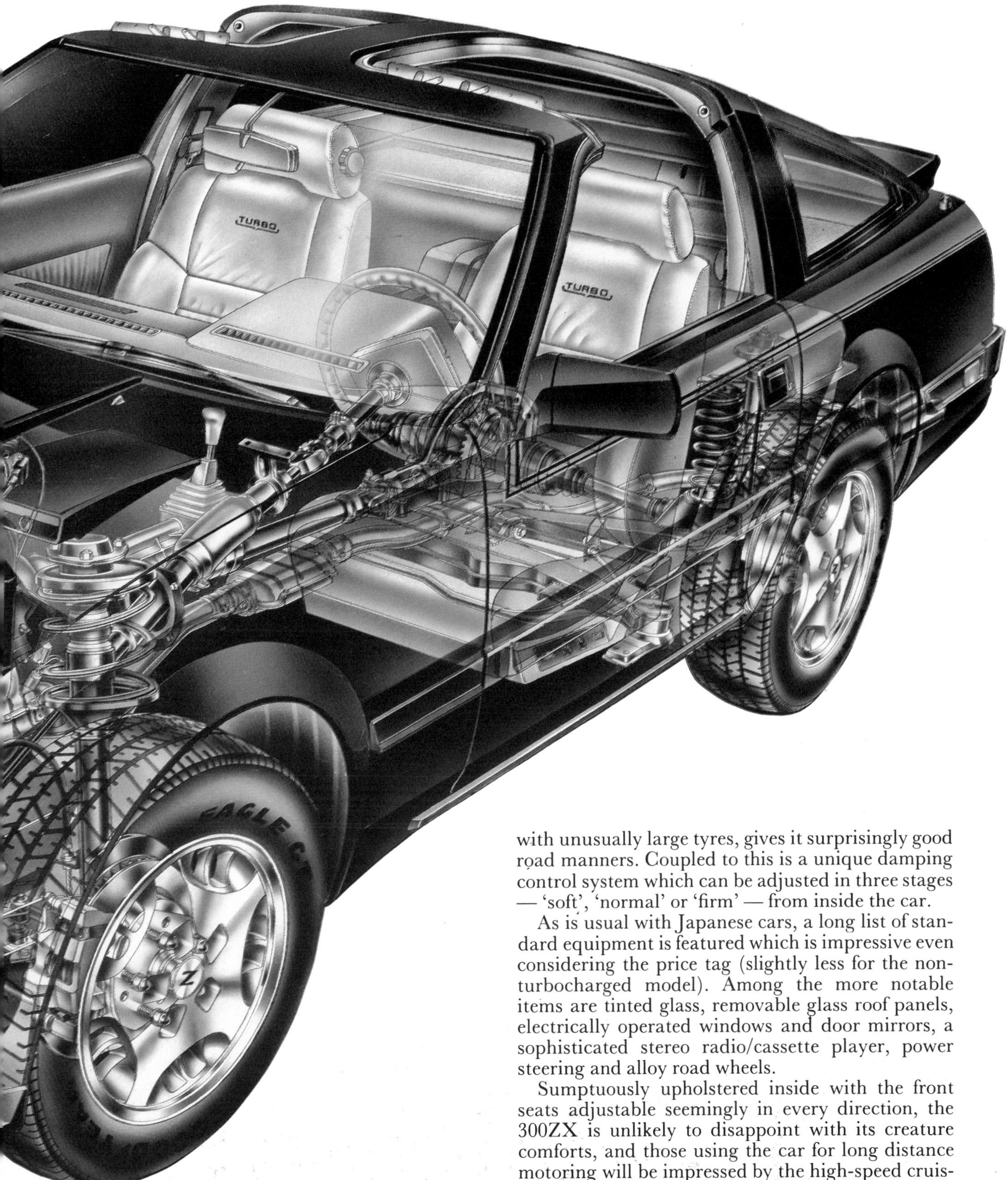

Softening up of the 'Z car' image in recent years has brought about changes in the handling which make the car more at home on the motorway than on twisting country lanes, but the 300ZX has retained its basically competent MacPherson strut front/semi-trailing arm rear suspension which, together with unusually large tyres, gives it surprisingly good road manners. Coupled to this is a unique damping control system which can be adjusted in three stages — 'soft', 'normal' or 'firm' — from inside the car.

As is usual with Japanese cars, a long list of standard equipment is featured which is impressive even considering the price tag (slightly less for the non-turbocharged model). Among the more notable items are tinted glass, removable glass roof panels, electrically operated windows and door mirrors, a sophisticated stereo radio/cassette player, power steering and alloy road wheels.

Sumptuously upholstered inside with the front seats adjustable seemingly in every direction, the 300ZX is unlikely to disappoint with its creature comforts, and those using the car for long distance motoring will be impressed by the high-speed cruising ability but dismayed by the lack of luggage space. The enormous spare wheel unfortunately takes up 90 per cent of the boot space and it is only with the rear seats folded that an appreciable quantity of goods can be carried.

Despite its obvious shortcomings, there can be no doubt that the Nissan 300ZX is a sleek and stylish grand touring car that makes the choice in this very competitive sector of the market a difficult one.

PORSCHE 356

1948–1965

Although the 356 was the 356th design to be completed by the Porsche Büro, since it was set up in 1930, this one was different: the first car to carry the Porsche name.

The first car was a neat little open two-seater (spyder) which was completed in 1948. It was similar to a VW-based sports car project Ferdinand Porsche had designed before the Second World War, and thus it could be regarded as the only Porsche car in which he had any involvement (although he simply approved the project, and execution of the design was left to his son Ferry). The first cars used VW torsion bar suspension and the VW flat four 1,131 cc (69 cu in) pushrod ohv engine. This was mounted ahead of the rear axle line in the very first car, but all subsequent 356s had their engine behind the rear axle. This did nothing to offset the sudden oversteer that the swing axle rear suspension could induce, when the wheels tended to tuck in as weight transfer took effect during hard cornering, and which tended to catch out unwary drivers.

The claimed power output of the first engines was no more than 40 bhp, so the clean aerodynamics of the body were crucial to the car's maximum speed of 140 km/h (85 mph). This 1.1 litre engine was listed until 1954, but 1.3- and 1.5-litre engines had been

Above: *Original 356 Spyder* **Left:** *Later 356 coupé*

introduced in 1951. These gave up to 70 bhp, and from the following year power was transmitted through a synchromesh gearbox.

The 356A of 1955 was a unitary construction car, five engine options in varying states of tune within the two capacities of 1.3- and 1.6-litres were offered, and a version which gained widespread publicity was the short-lived Speedster. This was soon superseded at the top end of the range by the first Porsche dubbed 'Carrera', which was also the first production Porsche to be fitted with disc brakes.

The 356B range ran from 1959 until 1963, with sub-designations which related to engine power outputs—60, 75, 90 and Super 90—while the Carrera gained a 1,966 cc (120 cu in) 130 bhp engine in 1961. The 356C lasted for only two years, and there were only two basic models in the range, before it gave way to the 911 (this car was anticipated in some external aspects of late 356s).

The 356 was of course the model that launched Porsche into motor sport, very much part of the company history at all levels ever since. Private owners started competing with their 356s in the late 1940s, but the first works-entered car did not appear in a major event until 1951, when three were prepared for the Le Mans 24-hour Race. One started, with a 48 bhp version of the engine—a far cry from later turbocharged Porsches—and it won its class. In the same year a 1.5-litre coupe was third in the Liege-Rome-Liege, that extraordinary cross between a rally and an old-fashioned city-to-city race.

Many successes followed, and as Porsche became increasingly involved in motor sport the 356 series reached its ultimate form in the Carrera GTL, built with the collaboration of the Italian specialist firm Abarth, with smooth lightweight bodies. But it was through the standard 356 coupes on the roads of the world that Porsche became an internationally respected marque, and 356s are eagerly sought.

PORSCHE 911

1964 ONWARD

Clearly following Porsche's established design policy when it was introduced in 1964, the Porsche 911 typified the marque through two decades.

Ten years after it appeared one of many variants was the famous Turbo. Another ten years on and rumours that its by-then unfashionable rear-engined format meant that its discontinuation was imminent were firmly squashed by a factory spokesman, who looked forward to the 1994 versions . . .

The car was first seen as the 901 in 1963, the 911 designation coming as it was put into production in the following year. Inevitably—or so it seemed then—it had an air-cooled engine, a sohc flat six of 1,991 cc (122 cu in), which was rated at 130 bhp. In Porsche fashion, this overhung the back axle line; it drove through a five-speed manual gearbox. The 911

The 1984 Porsche Carrera 'Turbo-Look'

had MacPherson strut IFS, using torsion bars, while trailing arm and torsion bar independent suspension was used at the rear. The car thus had handling characteristics typical of Porsches of the early period, calling for circumspection from drivers not thoroughly familiar with them. The suspension was to be revised through the car's career, the first step in the transformation of its handling qualities coming with the 911S in 1966 while on later cars wider and more effective tyres made for a significant improvement.

Among many other developments, a 2,195 cc (134 cu in) 190 bhp engine came in 1969, a 2,341 cc (143 cu in) unit in 1971, a 2,687 cc (165 cu in) 210 bhp engine in 1973 and a 2,994 cc (183 cu in) development in 1977. By that time the Turbo had been introduced (in 1974), with 260 bhp from the first 3-litre engine, then 300 bhp from the 3,299 cc (202 cu in) version that came in 1978, to give the Turbo a maximum speed of around 260 km/h (160 mph). In racing trim, the turbo engine produced well over 600 bhp.

As far as external appearance were concerned, the first significant variant was the Targa of 1965, a convertible with a distinctive type of roll-over bar (the name Targa was to become generic, as it was applied to other cars on similar lines). The competitions-orientated Carrera came in 1972, in RS, RSL (RS lightweight) and RST (RS touring) forms; in coupe or Targa guise it had a prominent rear aerofoil, while the 'supercar' Turbo had front air dam and wide wheels as well as rear aerofoil of impressive dimensions.

The 911 had been introduced as a touring car, but in the second half of the 1960s and through much of the 1970s its all-round competition qualities were proved, in rallies and races. Rally high points came with victories in the Monte Carlo Rally, in 1968 (Vic Elford), 1969–70 (Bjorn Waldegaard) and 1978 (Jean-Pierre Nicolas). On the circuits the leading teams in Europe were run by the Kremer brothers and George Loos—their cars dominated the GT classes through to the mid-1970s—while in the USA Carreras were very successful in the Camel GT and TransAm championships, while an RSR won the Daytona 24 hours as recently as 1977. The Turbo racing successes—and they were even more numerous—were joint second with the 935, which came to be regarded as the racing 'partner' to the 911 Turbo.

That 1977 Daytona victory, together with Nicholas' in the 1978 Monte Carlo Rally, underline the evergreen qualities of the 911. These were certainly appreciated by a generation of Porsche customers, who could have chosen much later front-engined designs.

Right: *Porsche 935, the racing development of the 911 Turbo, which has been very successful in the late 1970s and 1980s*

Below right: *Standard 911 Turbo which despite extended wheel arches and rear spoiler still retains the fast shape of the original 911*

Below: *Porsche 911 Targa which, until the recently introduced convertible, was the only open-topped 911*

MARTINI PORSCHE
Shell
1
BILSTEIN
BOSCH
Shell
DUNLOP
MARTINI
YJH 122T

PORSCHE 928

1977 ONWARD

The critics said that Porsche had at last got it wrong with the 928 when the performance of the 4.5-litre V8 car didn't live up to expectations. Porsche's answer was the 928S which really is a supercar in every sense of the word.

Announced in 1977, the gestation period of the 928 was at least seven years and the concept stemmed from Porsche's perception of the way motoring would develop over the course of the next twenty years at least. With that in mind, the 928 was designed with provision for meeting every aspect of safety legislation that Porsche could forsee. Despite this, the car arrived with a large-displacement V8 engine rather than the small capacity turbocharged unit that one might have predicted for a supercar of the future.

Porsche had certainly succeeded completely in taming the 911, which in theory had an appalling basic design, so another rear engined or mid-engined car might have been expected as the 911's replacement, for that is what the 928 seemed at first to be. Of course, it was, as it turned out, in no way a replacement, as the 911 lives on with seemingly undiminished appeal. Quite unlike the 911, the 928 had a front-mounted engine driving the rear wheels through a transaxle. What's more, the engine was water cooled, in itself an innovation for Porsche whose cars to date, with the exception of the then-new 924, had been air-cooled.

The V8 engine was linked solidly to a rear-mounted gearbox, an arrangement that gives a very favourable weight distribution and associated handling benefits. Power output of the 928's light alloy fuel-injected engine was 240 bhp which meant that the unit was fairly lightly stressed. Customers could choose between a five-speed manual gearbox or a three-speed automatic unit.

The 928's body was startlingly sleek and free from adornments, with the rear bumpers hidden behind a curvaceous deformable plastic panel. No aerodynamic aids spoilt the car's smooth line. The body was executed in steel with aluminium doors, bonnet and rear hatch.

Despite having a top speed of 225 km/h (140 mph) and acceleration to 60 mph in around 7.5 seconds,

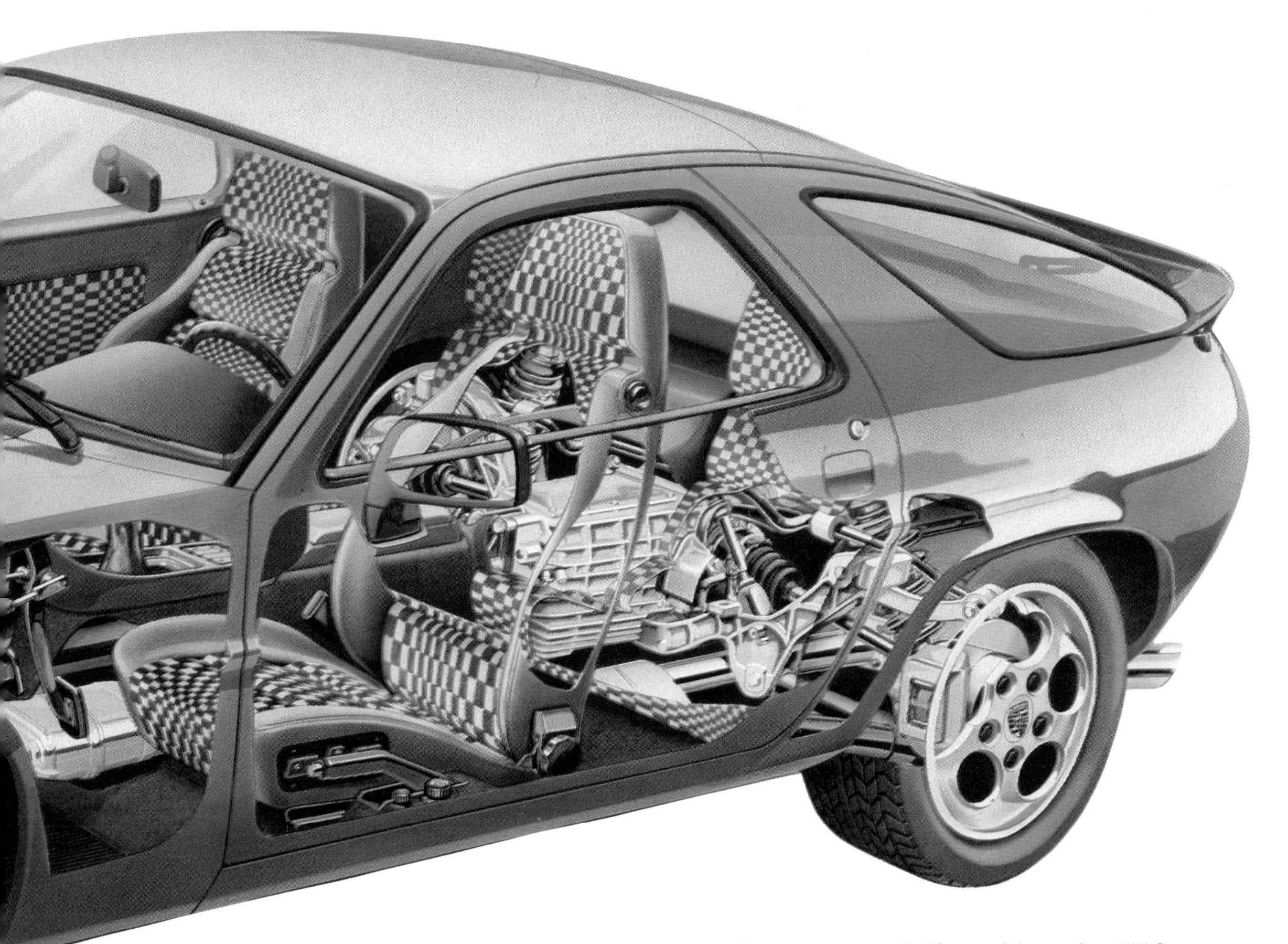

the 928 was deemed by many reviewers to be a disappointment, both performance-wise and aesthetically.

Porsche answered these critics in 1981 by introducing the 928S with an engine enlarged to 4.7-litres (286 cu in) and producing considerably more power. In addition the new version had a discreet rear spoiler and a chin spoiler at the front. Other points of difference were the side rubbing strip, different pattern wheels and alternative size Pirelli P7 tyres.

Top speed of the 928S was boosted at a stroke to 258 km/h (160 mph) and acceleration was similarly improved to real supercar specification. Few people had found fault with the 928's handling and general road manners and, if anything, the 928S was even better in these respects. Even those who had faulted the 928's styling had to admit that a liking for the car's looks came with time while, of course, most people loved it right from the start.

The 928S is ranked with the Ferraris, Maseratis and Lamborghinis of this world, but the significant difference between it and these other elitist vehicles is that the Porsche is made in quite large numbers and its quality, reliability and, arguably, its engineering integrity is higher. Few people would, or more importantly *could*, use any of the other supercars as everyday transport, yet the 928 adapts to this role quite readily, making it quite probably the most practical and maybe therefore the most satisfying supercar around.

RILEY 1½ LITRE

1945–1955

Announced in late August 1945, the RMA Series Riley, better known as the Riley 1½-litre, was a good-looking and sleek car.

Initially, it was built at the old Riley Motor Manufacturing Company's premises at Foleshill in Coventry, although the company had been taken over by Nuffield Motors in 1938 after the Riley Company had got into financial difficulties: the last ties of the Riley name with its founding town came in 1949, when production of the 1½ was moved to the M.G. factory at Abingdon. Eventually, by 1956, Riley no longer had a separate identity, for the cars became merely Wolseleys with the addition of twin SU carburettors.

The Riley 1½-litre was a good-looking car with a lean and purposeful appearance with its vee radiator (the radiator cap was a dummy), long swept wings, fabric-covered roof and well-shaped tail. The engine was virtually the pre-war 16 hp four-cylinder unit that had powered earlier Rileys, but it had been modified so that the drive to the twin camshafts was by means of a chain, rather than by the gears used earlier. As was traditional in Rileys, the camshafts were set high in the cylinder block and operated the overhead valves through short pushrods. Also traditional were the hemispherical combustion chambers, cross-flow ports and SU carburettors.

The car weighed about 1,322 kg (2,912 lb) and the 1,496 cc (91 cu in) engine produced no more than 55 bhp so the car was by no means quick or sporty. Acceleration from 0 to 96 km/h (0 to 60 mph) took almost 31 seconds, and the top speed was a modest 121 km/h (75 mph): those who desired more performance could always opt for the 2½-litre Riley, the stablemate of the 1½.

The chassis, like many earlier Rileys, was separate from the bodywork and featured torque-tube transmission and a large live rear axle mounted on semi-elliptic springs; the front suspension arrangement, however, broke away from earlier Riley practice and featured independent wishbones and torsion bars.

This suspension arrangement, together with the long wheelbase—285 cm (9 ft 4.5 in) in an overall body length of 455 cm (14 ft 11 in)—and a low centre of gravity made for stable handling, and the rack-and-pinion steering was precise, if somewhat heavy. Drum brakes were fitted to all four wheels, and the 25.4 cm (10 in) diameter units gave adequate retardation. The brakes on early models were hydraulically operated at the front and mechanically operated at the rear.

During 1948, the floor pan of the 1½ was lowered to make more passenger space inside the car, and the bonnet sides were adapted so that access to the engine, which had previously been very limited, was improved. Further changes took place in 1951, when the original two-piece bumpers were changed for full-width units at the front and the rear, and in the next year the rear window was enlarged, the brakes were changed to full hydraulic actuation, and the torque tube was replaced by a two-piece prop shaft. In 1953 the running boards were removed and the long mudguards changed for shorter shell-shaped ones.

Production ceased in 1955, by which time 11,854 Series RMA and 2,096 of the later Series RME models had been built, giving a total of 13,950 cars.

ROLLS-ROYCE CORNICHE

1971 ONWARD

When it was introduced in the Spring of 1971, this car was reviewed as the ultimate Rolls-Royce, although that aspect took second place to speculation about the company's fortunes, which had suffered a devastating setback.

However, the car division survived and prospered, in part because the Corniche was a success, and in turn was to be followed by other successes—Silver Wraith II, Silver Spirit and Bentleys among them.

The Corniche was seen as a superior derivative of the Silver Shadow, and had perhaps the best-balanced lines of any large cars of the 1970s. In its restrained convertible form it was an appreciating asset while it was still in production. The Silver Shadow had been announced in 1965, breaking new ground for Rolls-Royce—it was the first of the marque to have a monocoque body, all-independent suspension (with self-levelling height control), four-wheel disc braking, and detail 'novelties'. One of the few major components carried over from it predecessor was the V8, in 6,750 cc (412 cu in) form. This was also used in the Corniche, uprated to produce some 10 per cent more power, due to refinements such as new air cleaning arrangements, larger-bore exhaust pipes and revised camshaft profile. Rolls-Royce never state the power output of one of their engines, but in this case educated estimates suggested 240–250 bhp (whatever the figure, it was to be reduced to little more than 200 bhp by exhaust emission regulations). Transmission was through the sophisticated General Motors three-speed automatic gearbox.

The integral body and chassis was in sheet steel, with light alloy doors and similar fitments. Suspension was independent, with wishbones and coil spring/damper units at the front, and semi-trailing arms and coil spring/damper units at the rear, where there was also automatic hydraulic ride height control (from 1979 hydropneumatic struts). Ventilated disc brakes were fitted at the front, plain discs at the rear. The suspension was regularly refined, with greater revisions in 1976 and alterations to its geometry in 1980. Rack and pinion steering replaced the less-than-satisfactory recirculating ball type in 1976.

The interior was fitted naturally to high standards of luxury, with a very complex heating and air conditioning system controlled by sensors. Automatic cruise control was a standard fitting. These were heavy cars, the saloon weighing 2,258 kg (4,978 lb) unladen, while strengthening plates, heavier door posts, soft-top mechanism and so on brought the weight of the convertible up to 2,324 kg (5,124 lb). The maximum speed of 193 km/h (120 mph) was therefore creditable, while the manner in which it was silently achieved was admirable. There was naturally a penalty in fuel consumption, which averaged almost 24 litres/100 km (around 12 mpg) on the early cars. Economy was hardly expected to be uppermost in the minds of Rolls-Royce customers, but Rolls-Royce was to be worried by US requirements and the range with a 107 litre (23.5 Imp gallon) fuel tank was only just adequate for a car in this class.

That, however, was a minor drawback, for the Corniche was a car of great elegance and refinement, especially in the convertible version which outlived the saloon. This was one of the few cars of its time which bestowed prestige on its owner.

ROVER P4

1949–1964

Rover's first all-new model after the Second World War, the 75 P4, appeared in October 1949 and was the forerunner of a series of soundly constructed, robustly engineered saloon cars that found favour with professional men.

Initially, a distinctive frontal treatment was employed, with a single fog lamp mounted centrally in the radiator grille, earning the model the soubriquet 'Cyclops'. On all subsequent models a vertically-slatted grille was substituted.

In those days Rovers were more idiosyncratic than their current counterparts, the P4s featuring internal running boards (visible only with the doors open), rear doors hinged on their trailing edges to facilitate access, a shepherd's crook handbrake and a curious and complicated remote-control gear change mechanism with a long, cranked lever running back from the actual operational point; the very early cars featured an equally tortuous steering column change while some of the 60, 75 and 90 models were fitted with a free-wheel.

The 75 had a six-cylinder engine of 2,103 cc (128 cu in) which used an F-head configuration. Power output was a modest 75 bhp at 4,200 rpm. The robust chassis had a 280 cm (9 ft 3 in) wheelbase, the tracks were both 130 cm (4 ft 4 in) and with an overall length just under 455 cm (15 ft) the car weighed 1,407 kg (3,100 lb). The 60 and 80 cars used four-cylinder engines, while the 90, 95, 100, 105 and 110 models used six-cylinder units of 2.6-litre (158 cu in) capacity which in the 110 was rated at 123 bhp at 5,000 rpm. Front suspension was independent by coil springs, and semi-elliptic leaf springs were used on the live rear axle. Brakes were operated hydraulically at the front and mechanically at the rear of early cars; later models used hydraulics all round with discs at the front.

With its predominantly forward weight distribution the P4 called for skilful handling at speed while the recirculating ball steering required very considerable effort during low speed manoeuvring. The original 75, retailing at £1,106, could attain 137 km/h (85 mph) and reach 81 km/h (50 mph) from rest in 15.6 seconds; fuel consumption was never better than 10.4 litres/100 km (27 mpg), even on the later overdrive cars. The 110 had a maximum speed of just over 160 km/h (100 mph).

All P4s featured sumptuous interiors with walnut and leather and comfortable seating for five or six adults in the rather dignified style that had become a Rover hallmark. The model was a success for the company. It was very reliable, well-equipped and epitomized the best in British engineering; not for nothing was it known as the 'poor man's Rolls-Royce'. Staid and solid, some 130,342 P4s were produced between October 1949 and May 1964, when the model was superseded by the larger P5 which had run in parallel since it was introduced in 1958 and more advanced P6 Rovers. As with many cars of this period, the Rover P4 and P5 have now become highly collectable, partly due to their strong construction and durability.

Rover 90. The 'poor man's Rolls-Royce'

STUDEBAKER AVANTI

1962–1963

An exciting car by the standards of the American industry in the 1960s, the sleek Avanti was a last brave attempt to stave off the end of more than sixty years of car production by a famous old company.

Studebaker had entered the 1960s with the Hawk and Lark lines, straightforward models with V8 and straight-six engines, and undistinguished specifications and bodies. Much of the engineering was carried over to the Avanti, but when it was introduced in 1962 (for 1963) this model had the first new body styling on a Studebaker since 1953. And it was this body that made the new car stand out in a crowd, for in its lines it was years ahead of it contemporaries from Detroit.

It was the work of a team headed by Raymond Loewy, who had been responsible for the early Hawks, and of necessity it had to be ready for production very quickly. This was also a prime reason for the selection of fibreglass as the body material. Basically, it had 'coke-bottle' lines, and despite the lack of wind tunnel tests the body proved to be as aerodynamically efficient as it was visually attractive. There was only one style, effectively a four-seater GT sedan, with little ornamentation, although in the fascia Lowey did consciously ape aircraft instruments and controls.

The running gear came from the Hawk, with anti-roll bars added front and rear, while the chassis was a shortened version of rather flexible frame used for the Lark Daytona convertible. Together with some Hawk and Lark models, the Avanti was one of the first US production models to be fitted with disc brakes, using the Dunlop-type Bendix at the front.

The engine was the standard Studebaker 4,736 cc (289 cu in) pushrod ohv V8 which in the normal R1 form was rated at 240 bhp. The R2 had a Paxton supercharger, and appropriate modifications such as different camshafts and carburettors, and it developed 290 bhp. Slightly larger (305 cu in) versions were intended for the Avanti, while a car was fitted with the fuel-injected, twin-supercharged R5 and used by Andy Granatelli to break stock records at Bonneville.

Apart from that episode the Avanti's potential was not proved, and problems with the fibreglass body manufacturer meant that it was dropped before the company ceased production at South Bend in the USA in 1963, and it was not among the models continued in production (with Chevrolet engines) at Studebaker's Canadian plant for another two years.

However, part of the old South Bend factory, together with the rights to the Avanti, dies, parts, etc, was acquired by a local dealer, who resumed modest production of the car, using Avanti II as a make name. Some of the fibreglass problems that had hampered production of the original were avoided as bodies were bought-in from the company that produced Corvette bodies. The Corvette V8 was also fitted, from 1965 until 1970 in 5,358 cc (327 cu in) 300 bhp form, and in 1971–72 in 5,735 cc (350 cu in) 270 bhp form; as emission controls emasculated engines a still larger GM V8 of 6,554 cc (400 cu in) was adopted, in an attempt to maintain performance. Although details such as bumpers had to change, uprated in response to the demands of safety legislation, the appearance of the Avanti II remained close to the original, and in some respects these 'replicars' were more highly rated than Studebaker's last classic design.

SUNBEAM-TALBOT 90

1948–1957

Many enthusiasts for post-Second World War cars rate the Sunbeam-Talbot 90 as the best car produced under that marque name.

The Sunbeam/Talbot names, incidentally, go back separately to the origins of the motor industry, and were linked again with the revival of the Talbot name for the Chrysler Europe company acquired in 1978 by the PSA Peugeot-Citroen group.

The 90 had humble origins in the pre-war Hillman Minx and yet with steady and consistent development became a handsome sporting car. Despite quite serious drawbacks (such as a column gear change which was poor even by the modest standards of the late 1940s), it attracted drivers such as Stirling Moss, Mike Hawthorn and Sheila van Damm to enter major international rallies, and to achieve some notable successes.

The names Sunbeam and Talbot had been acquired by the Rootes family in the early 1930s: the Rootes company did not start as car manufacturers, but was a sales organization which over a fairly short period bought ailing car companies and built them into a large group (their acquisitions included Hillman, Humber and Singer, in addition to Sunbeam and Talbot). Rootes launched the Minx Aero in 1933 and three years later used that car's underslung chassis as the basis for the Talbot 10, a very attractive car notable for its pillarless rear quarters which were to remain a feature of the marque for 21 years. The name Sunbeam was added in 1938, and in 1939 virtually the same body appeared as the '2-litre', fitted with a Hillman 14 engine. Production of these models resumed after the Second World War, and the 80 and 90 models were announced in 1948.

This was the first appearance of what is now recognized as a classic shape, but the 80 model was dropped after only two years as with only 1,185 cc (71 cu in) to power it, performance was acceptable to a very few people—about 3,500 80s were built.

The 90 was a great deal more popular, and the Mark II, introduced at the London Motor Show in 1950, had a new version of the overhead valve Hillman engine, bored out to 2,267 cc (138 cu in), and a vastly improved chassis incorporating independent front suspension for the first time. The Mark IIA, introduced in 1952, had better gearing and brakes and the appearance of the car was improved by raising the headlamps and dispensing with the 'spats' in the rear wheel arches.

From its inception, the 90 had been available either as a four-door saloon, or as a two-door coupe, but it took a Rootes dealer, George Hartwell, to show how a handsome open two-seater could be made, and in 1953 the manufacturers produced their own version, called the Alpine.

The following year saw some major changes: the name Talbot was dropped for a Mark III version which had overdrive as an optional extra, and engine developments that provided a higher output of 80 bhp. Later an Alpine 'Special' became available, and this was the most powerful of all the 90s, with a new high compression ratio of 8:1, a claimed output of 97.5 bhp and a top speed of over 160 km/h (100 mph). Production of the 90 continued until 1957; in all, some 25,000 were built.

SUNBEAM TIGER

1965–1967

More than one sports car has successfully combined a large American V8 engine with a lightweight British body and chassis, and among road cars (as opposed to racers) the Sunbeam Tiger was one of the best.

Very fast and with handling that could prove vicious in unskilled hands, only a sympathetic driver could truly appreciate the Tiger's special virtues and could come to love the car.

Sadly, it had a very short production life. Carroll Shelby and Ken Miles were commissioned by Ian Garrad, son of the former Rootes Group competitions manager, to build two prototypes in 1962. After some further develpments, two cars ran at Le Mans in 1964, and production proper started in March 1965. The original Tiger 260s were fitted with Ford of Detroit 4.3-litre Fairlane engines, but in late 1966 the Tiger 260 had to be replaced by the 4.7-litre Tiger 289 when Ford dropped the 4.3-litre unit. (The Tiger type numbers denote the engine capacities in cubic inches.) The 289 remained in production only six months, for the Rootes Group had meanwhile been taken over by Chrysler, and they could hardly continue selling a Ford-engined car.

The Tiger had very mixed origins. Its 4,261 cc (260 cu in) cast-iron engine and four-speed manual gearbox came directly from America, and the two-seater Sunbeam Alpine body (which was made by Pressed Steel) was modified by Jensen, who did the actual assembly work. Compared to the Alpine, it had re-shaped toeboards (giving slightly less leg-room), rack-and-pinion steering on a new front cross-member, heavier springs and dampers, a Panhard rod to the rear axle, a higher (2.88:1) final drive and twin exhausts. Other changes included a cross-flow radiator with header tank, and repositioning of the battery, which now was fitted in the boot.

With almost twice the power and three times the torque of the ordinary Sunbeam Alpine (although the weight was also increased by some 193 kg/448 lb), acceleration was impressive by the standards of the mid-1960s: 0 to 100 km/h (0 to 60 mph) took just over 9 seconds, and the top speed was not far short of 190 km/h (120 mph). Unwary drivers could easily be caught out by the tail of the car, which was liable to swing out of line whether the road surface was wet or dry, and the brakes, being unchanged from those of the Alpine, were barely adequate. Because the Tiger was designed primarily for the smooth-surfaced American roads, the chassis and suspension was a little 'busy' on rougher surfaces, such as those encountered in the UK. Early models suffered from some lack of body rigidity, but this fault was soon eliminated. The later 4,737 cc (290 cu in) Tiger 289 was considerably faster: a contemporary road test on a mildly-tuned example showed a top speed of 201 km/h (125 mph) and a 0 to 100 km/h (0 to 62 mph) time of just 7.8 seconds. The 289 was improved in detail, but still remained some way short of perfection in terms of its road behaviour. In all, 7,002 production models were built, of which 6,468 were model 260s and 534 were model 289s.

TRIUMPH ROADSTER

1946–1949

When Sir John Black took over the Triumph company towards the end of the Second World War, he had a special convertible built for his own use, and liked it so much that he decided to market it as a production model.

Mechanically the recipe was simple enough: a shortened version of the tubular chassis used for the 1800 saloon, complete with Standard's pre-war transverse leaf independent front suspension, and the pushrod OHV version of the 1,776 cc (108 cu in) Standard 14 hp engine which he supplied to SS and Jaguar for their four-cylinder models.

What made the Triumph Roadster so refreshing in a dismal post-war world was its unusual styling, which could be described as a revival of the classic dual-cowl phaetons produced by top coachbuilders in the 1930s. It was a perfectly practical open car that could carry two or even three on its wide bench seat, and another two in a 'dickey' seat behind. Winding glass windows and a well-made hood kept the cockpit snug in poor weather, while the dickey seat passengers were reasonably well protected by their own separate windscreen, which folded down to form part of the boot lid when not in use.The long, tapering bonnet was fronted by a neat radiator, set some way back between deeply valanced front wings which carried relatively large headlamps. Not everybody liked the Roadster's looks, but it was an ingenious piece of styling and invariably attracted attention.

It was also a well-finished car, verging almost on the luxurious, and exceptionally comfortable to drive on long journeys, open or closed—especially when framed windows were fitted together with an improved hood.

But it was certainly not a sports car, with an engine giving only 65 bhp, a high-drag shape and considerable frontal area, not to mention the dry weight of nearly 1,169 kg (2,576 lb). Acceleration was unimpressive, and very few Roadsters would exceed or even reach 130 km/h (80 mph) in standard tune. This was just as well, for if better performance had been available the combination of doubtful roadholding and vague, low-geared steering might have put some drivers in trouble. Although Girling hydrostatic self-adjusting brakes worked well, they were too small for their task and thus wore rapidly, while the steering column gear change was as unsatisfactory as most of its kind.

From late 1948 the Triumph Roadster was equipped with the Standard Vanguard's rugged 2,088 cc (127 cu in) four-cylinder engine and three-speed gearbox, while the rear axle was changed from spiral bevel to hypoid design.

With 68 bhp and less weight than earlier models, the 2000's acceleration and fuel consumption were improved, but strengthening the frame failed to eradicate some scuttle shake. Maximum speed was virtually unchanged, though there was a slight fall in top-end acceleration. The loss of one gear made little difference, for the Vanguard engine was a flexible unit, and the new second gear actually allowed a higher speed than the third gear of the earlier unit.

The Triumph Roadster possessed rakish looks that belied its true performance and by 1949 Triumph were hard at work on the prototype of the model that subsequently became the TR2, an altogether different car, and Roadster production came to an end during that year.

TRIUMPH TR3

1955–1961

If a car can be said to sum up the feel of an era, the Triumph TR must be a good candidate for the car of the 1950s.

A TR was then the 'car to have' for the hard-driving sporting motorist who couldn't quite aspire to the heights of expensive Jaguar XKs or Austin -Healeys. Discomfort, water leaks, draughts and noise were in most people's eyes a small price to pay for the TR's snappy acceleration, its top speed of over 160 km/h (100 mph) and its safe, predictable handling.

Standard Triumph recovered quickly after the Second World War and in 1946 announced their first post-war sporting model, the 1800 Roadster. This was a moderate success, but shortcomings in the Roadster's design began to show severely by 1949 and production soon ceased. Standard Triumph set about designing a replacement within the constraints of a very small budget.

Eventually a 'Triumph Sports Prototype' was exhibited at the 1952 Motor Show in London. The car utilized many components from existing models and had a distinctive 'dumpy' body which was also a feature of the later TRs. The design was dictated as much by the cheapness of producing the simple rounded panels as by design philosophy. However, initial tests soon showed up serious weaknesses in the prototype and a rapid development programme ensued, resulting in an extensive re-design which was unveiled at the 1953 Geneva Motor Show. The TR2, as the new car became known, went into production in August 1953. It featured an immensely strong four-cylinder, wet linered, OHV engine of 1,991 cc (121 cu in) capacity which, fitted with twin SU carburettors, produced 90 bhp at 4,800 rpm. The car's four-speed gearbox had the useful option of an overdrive unit which initially operated only on fourth gear but subsequently on second and third. The front suspension was independent with coil springs while the rear featured a live axle with semi-elliptic springs.

The car's specification endowed it with sparkling performance with a top speed of 165 km/h (103 mph), coupled with sporting handling and remarkable fuel consumption of 9 litres/100 km (30 mpg). It soon became apparent that the TR was an ideal car for the private competitor and in both racing and rallying TRs, often little modified, took honour after honour. In cases where overall victory was elusive, the rugged, reliable TRs generally took class honours. Works TRs also met with international success with strong showings in events such as the Le Mans 24-hour Race and the French Alpine Rally.

Sales of the TR2 continued apace and in 1955 the TR3 was introduced. In reality this was little different from the TR2, but featured a more powerful engine with enlarged inlet ports and bigger carburettors. In addition, the front of the car received an egg-box grill to replace the TR2's gaping 'mouth'. A further change came in August 1956 when, among other things, the TR3 was fitted with front disc brakes, a more modified engine which now produced 100 bhp at 5,000 rpm, a stronger rear axle and a full width front grill. Although popularly known as the TR3A, the car was never known as such by the factory. The car's price remained extremely competitive and sales expanded greatly, especially in export markets as indicated by the production totals for the TR2/3/3A of 80,341, of which 74,239 were exported, the majority to America. Although hardly thoroughbred machines, these early TRs are now much sought cars on both sides of the Atlantic.

VOLKSWAGEN 'BEETLE'

1945 ONWARD

British manufacturers had the opportunity to take over the design of the 'Beetle' at the close of the war but dismissed it as too idiosyncratic. Volkswagen went on to prove them wrong.

Volkswagen in Germany may have ceased production of the 'Beetle' having clocked up an amazing total of almost 20 million units built, but this remarkable car continues to be constructed elsewhere, notably in Brazil. Ironically a handful of cars are exported back to Europe each year to satisfy a demand that still exists.

The origins of the 'Beetle', which, it should be said, was never actually known as such officially, lie in pre-war Germany where Dr Ferdinand Porsche had schemed designs for several rear-engined cars, none of which reached the production stage. Encouraged by the Nazi government and almost certainly with a personal input from Adolf Hitler, Porsche pursued the design and oversaw the building of prototypes of the so-called 'people's car' in 1937. A factory designed for full-scale production was almost ready by the outbreak of war in 1939.

War prevented the start of production, but from 1939 until 1944, versions of the Volkswagen were built for military use. Only in 1945 did production of civilian versions start in earnest and thereafter the success of this cheap and strange but extraordinarily reliable and practical car seemed to know no bounds.

The first 'Beetles' were crude in the extreme, with a rear-mounted, air-cooled and seemingly unburstable four-cylinder engine of 1,131 cc (68 cu in). The handling was as peculiar as the car's appearance, but buyers soon came to terms with this, as they did with the minimal performance and luggage space.

As the years passed the 'Beetle' was constantly improved with changes being made to the engine which was progressively made larger, ending up at 1,600 cc (98 cu in); the gearbox, which received synchromesh; and the styling, the most notable change here being the enlarging of the initially tiny rear window. However, throughout the model's life, Volkswagen remained true to Dr Porsche's concept of the basic 'Beetle' and the changes they made were, in all honesty, not fundamental. The car's performance and handling, were definitely improved, but it was never more than average in these respects. But, the 'Beetle's' simplicity and its honest character meant there was always a ready market. Convertible versions and a sleeker-bodied Karmann Ghia design extended that market still further.

1947 Volkswagen 'Beetle', the peoples' car

VOLVO P444/P544

1944–1965

The Volvo PV444 was the first high-volume production car of the Swedish firm, and was a great success.

Aktiebolaget Volvo was founded in 1926 by two former colleagues of the Swedish ball-bearing company SKF. They began with their own capital, but so impressed SKF with their plans for careful assembly and high quality that the larger company was prevailed upon to provide both premises and financial support. By 1944, Volvo had established itself as a national car, truck and bus company, but in that year the company gave the first indication of it intention of also becoming a world producer.

The Volvo PV444 had somewhat odd American-influenced styling but, unlike its predecessors, it was quite small, with a four-cylinder overhead valve engine of only 1,414 cc (86 cu in) and a three-speed gearbox. Although narrow, the two-door round-tailed body was a full four-seater, providing a remarkable amount of space for four passengers and their luggage.

Three years were spent developing the PV444 as Volvo's first unitary construction, high-volume motor car. Production expanded rapidly after the initial launch in 1944; 2,000 were built in 1947, rising to a peak of 132,000 ten years later. In addition, between 1957 and 1958, a further 64,000 PV444s were marketed with a more powerful 1,583 cc (96 cu in) engine.

In 1958, the PV was given a facelift: the PV544, as the new model was known, kept the old lines, but a curved single-piece windscreen and revised frontal treatment gave the car a new look. A bigger, single rear window was fitted but, because of the huge boot aperture, this was still not really deep enough to provide the driver with adequate rearward vision. Unchanged on the new model were the solid construction and fairly simple mechanical elements.

The sporting character of the car was enhanced by a choice of single and twin carburettor specifications, the latter delivering a healthy 85 bhp. Some 134,000 PV544s were manufactured in the model's first three years, after which a 1,778 cc (108 cu in) engine was fitted which developed 95 bhp in the final, and most powerful example of the marque, the PV544S. A further 105,000 were produced in the 1.8-litre form, before the PV series was phased out just before the 144 range was launched; the PV was thus manufactured for many years alongside the 120 series cars that were designed originally to replace it. In fairness to the 120 series cars, however, it should be pointed out that these 'Amazon' style of Volvos were still being produced in 1970, and thus overlapped the 144 series by which, in turn, they were supposed to be superseded.

With its well-damped coil springing (that was independent at the front), its speed, handling and rigidity, the PV model proved itself to be a fine rally car, especially in rough 'stage' events. A PV444 won the Norwegian Viking rally three years running in 1957/8/9, the Midnight Sun—then the Swedish National rally—in 1957/8, and also Finland's Thousand Lakes in 1959.

In 1963 Tom Trana swept to victory in the RAC Rally in a PV544, and repeated that success in 1964, when he gave the model a new lease of competitive life by also taking the Acropolis and Midnight Sun rallies. Tom Trana and the 20-year old PV were undisputed European Champions of 1964, but there was one more major success to come: in its final production year, 1965, a PV544, driven by the Singh brothers, won outright the toughest of all rallies, the East African Safari, thus bringing the competition career of this car to a close on the highest note.

WOLSELEY 6/80

1948–1954

Unveiled at the 1948 Motor Show, the Wolseley 6/80 was very much the product of the Nuffield Group's post-war policy of continual rationalization, which eventually spelt *finis* for the marque's individuality.

It had the same monocoque body shell as the equally new Morris Six, except for a different bonnet and radiator. It even had the same six-cylinder overhead cam engine, but with an extra SU carburettor and slightly different gear ratios.

The 6/80 would carry five people in reasonable comfort on its leather seats, the front ones separate instead of bench-type even though the gear lever was mounted on the steering column in the fashion of the period. Front suspension was independent by wishbone and torsion bar, and the hypoid bevel rear axle was carried on semi-elliptic leaf springs, with Armstrong hydraulic dampers. Bishop cam steering was used, but this was inferior to the rack-and-pinion layout of the new Morris Minor, also seen for the first time at the 1948 show. The brakes were Lockheed drum, of two-leading-shoe type at the front. Interior decor and instruments were singularly uninspired, but the car was equipped with an interior heater, an unusual standard item in those days.

Two more unexpected devices were provided for starting and stopping the engine. There was an electric choke actuated by a knob on the fascia and another knob stopped the engine by closing the throttles completely—a reminder of the awful running-on that was common with low-octane Pool petrol when the ignition was switched off.

Pistons, con-rods, valves and many other parts were interchangeable with those of the four-cylinder OHC Nuffield engines, for they had all been designed with the same bore and stroke, excepting the side-valve Minor. The camshaft was driven by means of a vertical shaft instead of a chain, this at least being part of the Wolseley tradition, and had skew gears which were split and spring-loaded to prevent chattering. The valve stems were hollow, with internal threads in to which were screwed the adjustable mushroom tappets. The engine was lightly stressed, giving a mere 72 bhp at 4,600 rpm from its 2,215 cc (135 cu in) capacity.

With a hefty 1,300 kg (2,865 lb) of dry weight, the engine promised little in the way of performance. Although rated a lively car in its time, the Wolseley 6/80 was slower than almost any car of the 1980s, except of course the 'micro-cars', having a top speed of just under 130 km/h (80 mph) and a 0–100 km/h (0–60 mph) acceleration time of no less than 27.8 seconds. Fuel consumption was 14 litres/100 km (20 mpg) or worse.

Despite the above, however, the 6/80 was chosen as the police car of its day in succession to the Wolseley 18/85. For half-a-dozen years the enthusiastic British motorist watched his rear-view mirror for that familiar black shape, hoping to spot it before the front-mounted, chromium-plated electric gong sounded its ominous note, and, with true British sportsmanship, the illuminated Wolseley badge on the radiator of all police cars ensured that they could still be spotted in the mirror by an alert speeding motorist, even at night!

INDEX

Numbers in italics refer to illustrations

Picture Credits

Alfa Romeo Ltd: 52; Aston Martin Lagonda Ltd: 57, 101; Janette Beckman/Joe Bailey: 147; Barbara Bellingham: 69; British Leyland Cars Ltd: 59, 126; Neil Bruce: 18, 20, 21(b), 24(t), 36, 68; Diane Burnett: 45(t); Simon Butcher: 146; Citroen Cars Ltd: 42(t); Donald F. Clayton: 116; Steve Crawley: 9(c); Peter Dazeley: 31(b); Mirco Decet: 1, 2/3, 4/5, 48, 74/5, 77, 78, 95 ©British Leyland, 102/3, 103, 104, 117, 118/9, 132, 133, 148; F. H. Douglas/Jeff Wilkinson: 30; Fiat (Auto) Ltd: 80; G. N. Georgano: 37(b); Geoffrey Goddard: 8, 11(b), 16(t,b), 24(b), 34, 35(b), 43(b), Nelson Hargreaves: 140, H. Poynter/Riley RM Club, 144, J. Denmee/Sunbeam Talbot Alpine, 150 Wolsey Register/Alan Simmons; John Hillelson Agency/Lartigue: 26; David Hodges Collection: 84/5, 86/7; Jaguar Cars Ltd: 6(b), 22, 96/7, 98; James Johnson: 90; Louis Klementaski: 27(b); London Art Tech: 9(t), 10(t), 28/9, 46; Lotus Group of Companies: 115; John McGovren: 58, 62, 65, 66, 70, 120; Motor Sport Magazine; 33(b); Motor Trend/Petersen Publishing Co: 63, 64, 64/5, 88/9, 89(t,b), 130/1, P. Kimble 134, P. Kimble; Museum of British Road Transport (Coventry): 14, 23(b); National Motor Museum: 9(b), 17, 38(t), 39(r), 41(b), 82, 93, 99, 128; Newnes Books: 109, 110/1; Nostalgia: 49, 50/1; Pininfarina Ltd: 44; Charles Pocklington: 39(1), 91, 121; Porsche Cars Ltd: 136, 136/7, 138/9, 139; C. Posthumus: 19(t), 37(t), 47; Alan Ramsbottom: 142; Renault: 46/7; Peter Roberts: 6(t), 42(b), 45(b); Rolls Royce Ltd: 60, 141; SAAB Ltd: 11(t); Graham Sage: 67; Science Museum: 32(b); L. K. J. Settright: 61(1,r); Spectrum: 31(t); T & C C: 54, 72, 73, 113, 127; Colin Taylor Productions: 21(t), 29(1), 32(t); Mike Taylor/Tiger-Making of a Sports Car: 145; Tech-Del Ltd: 25; Trevor Vertigan: 56/7, 92/3, 114, 122; Amhurst Villiers: 13; Volvo AB Sweden: 149; Volvo Concessionairies Ltd: 41(t); Ted Waters/J. Twitty: 124; George Wright: 15(t), 83, 94, Z. Lisak, 108; Nicky Wright: 15(b), 40, 43(t), 76, 81; Zefa: 129.